TITANIC

TITA

RMS *TITANIC*'S SEA TRIALS, 6 AM ON TUESDAY, 2 APRIL 1912

ANIC

SEAN CALLERY

SCHOLASTIC *discover more*™

True Survivors' Stories

The dramatic events that took place on the night that *Titanic* sank are vividly brought to life through the personal accounts given by some of the survivors. Your free digital book features five of these incredible stories.

Your digital book is very simple to use. Enter the code (bottom right) to download it to any Mac or PC. Open it in Adobe Reader, also free to download. Then you're all set!

Harold Bride | Bruce Ismay | Violet Jessop

True Surv Stories
A digital companion to Titanic

Edith Rosenbaum

Edith Rosenbaum shivered. Her first-class cabin looked like a palace, but the heater didn't work, and she was freezing. At least it would be warm in the dining room. But what should she wear to dinner?

As a fashion designer and writer, Edith sold French fashions from Paris to the rich Americans who loved to travel on new liners. Like she had, many had joined *Titanic* at Cherbourg, France, on their way home from their European holidays. Among them was her millionaire friend John Jacob Astor, who declared the enormous ship to be "a modern miracle".

Maybe it was, but Edith preferred clothes to ships. She studied the elegant hats of the women as they watched their luggage being unloaded. Edith herself had so many trunks of dresses and coats that she had booked another cabin on E Deck just to store them in. The steward had been really helpful – he'd even found extra vases for the huge bunches of flowers that friends had sent to her cabin, then taken her thank-you messages to the radio room.

To Edith, the decision about what to wear at dinner was important – after all, *Titanic* was the most glamorous ship in the world. She eventually settled on a long white satin dress and a diamond necklace

Titanic was the most glamorous ship in the world.

that matched the diamond-studded buckles on her new shoes. She patted her lucky mascot – a little toy pig – and set off for the dining room.

Dinner that Sunday night was an elegant party at which beautifully dressed people ate the finest food and

laughed at witty conversation [...] smiled as she noticed how pe[...] their fashionable clothes mat[...] dining room's luxurious déco[...]

After dinner, she chose the [...] of the reading and writing ro[...] her cold cabin. She sat at a d[...] write about the dresses and s[...]

"Nothing to worry ab[...] We bumped into an ice[...] It's no problem at al[...]

had admired. At 11:30 PM, th[...] steward called, "Lights out", [...] handed him her letters to be [...]

"I'll pay for the stamps tomorrow," she said, then headed for her cabin. As her hand touched the door handle, Edith felt a strange bump, then another. She put on a fur coat and went out on deck to investigate.

[...] iceberg. It's no problem at all.

Edith was surprised she could hear his voice so clearly from so far away. Then she realized it was because the ship's engines had stopped. Something was wrong.

This toy pig was Edith Rosenbaum's lucky mascot. It contained a music box that played a tune when the pig's tail was wound.

Edith Rosenbaum
Fashion writer Edith boarded Lifeboat 11, where she wound the tail of her lucky toy pig to play music to comfort herself and others.

> **The babies were perpetually crying. I played my little musical pig to amuse them.**
>
> —EDITH ROSENBAUM, FIRST-CLASS PASSENGER

digital book

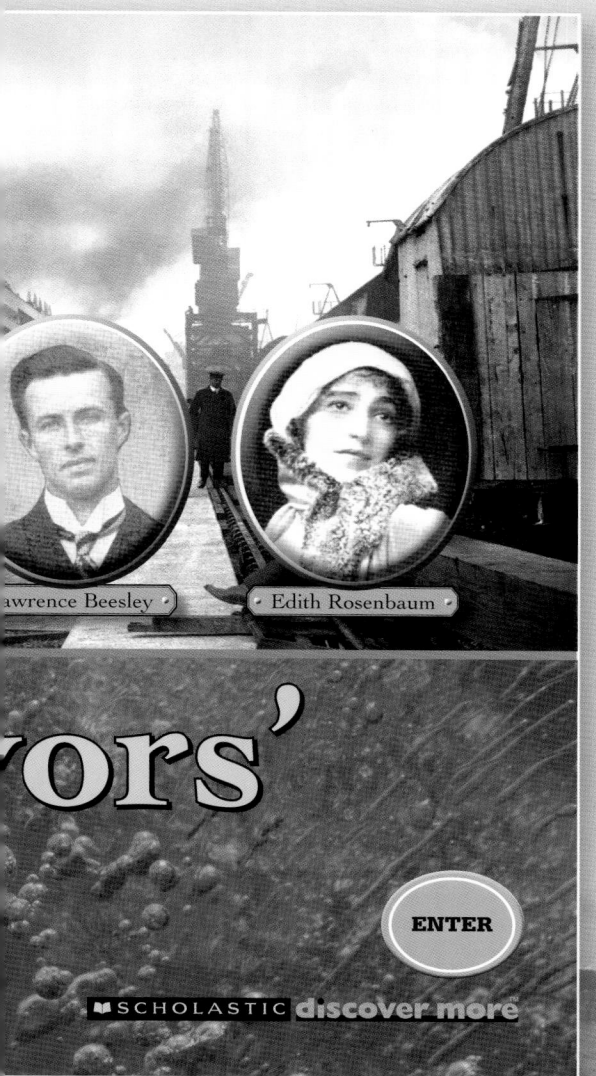

Lawrence Beesley | Edith Rosenbaum

ors'

ENTER

SCHOLASTIC discover more

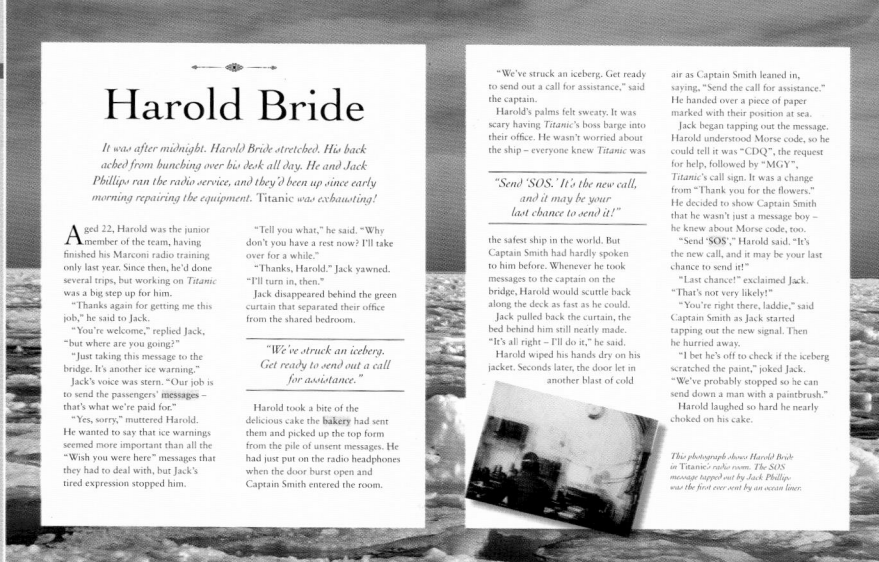

Harold Bride

It was after midnight. Harold Bride stretched. His back ached from hunching over his desk all day. He and Jack Phillips ran the radio service, and they'd been up since early morning repairing the equipment. Titanic was exhausting!

Aged 22, Harold was the junior member of the team, having finished his Marconi radio training only last year. Since then, he'd done several trips, but working on *Titanic* was a big step up for him.

"Thanks again for getting me this job," he said to Jack.

"You're welcome," replied Jack, "but where are you going?"

"Just taking this message to the bridge. It's another ice warning."

Jack's voice was stern. "Our job is to send the passengers' messages – that's what we're paid for."

"Yes, sorry," muttered Harold. He wanted to say that ice warnings seemed more important than all the "Wish you were here" messages that they had to deal with, but Jack's tired expression stopped him.

"Tell you what," he said. "Why don't you have a rest now? I'll take over for a while."

"Thanks, Harold." Jack yawned. "I'll turn in, then."

Jack disappeared behind the green curtain that separated their office from the shared bedroom.

"We've struck an iceberg. Get ready to send out a call for assistance."

Harold took a bite of the delicious cake the **bakery** had sent them and picked up the top form from the pile of unsent messages. He had just put on the radio headphones when the door burst open and Captain Smith entered the room.

"We've struck an iceberg. Get ready to send out a call for assistance," said the captain.

Harold's palms felt sweaty. It was scary having *Titanic*'s boss barge into their office. He wasn't worried about the ship – everyone knew *Titanic* was

"Send 'SOS'. It's the new call, and it may be your last chance to send it!"

the safest ship in the world. But Captain Smith had hardly spoken to him before. Whenever he took messages to the captain on the bridge, Harold would scuttle back along the deck as fast as he could.

Jack pulled back the curtain, the bed behind him still neatly made. "It's all right – I'll do it," he said.

Harold wiped his hands dry on his jacket. Seconds later, the door let in another blast of cold

air as Captain Smith leaned in, saying, "Send the call for assistance." He handed over a piece of paper marked with their position at sea.

Jack began tapping out the message. Harold understood Morse code, so he could tell it was "CQD", the request for help, followed by "MGY", *Titanic*'s call sign. It was a change from "Thank you for the flowers." He decided to show Captain Smith that he wasn't just a message boy – he knew about Morse code, too.

"Send 'SOS'," Harold said. "It's the new call, and it may be your last chance to send it!"

"Last chance!" exclaimed Jack. "That's not very likely!"

"You're right there, laddie," said Captain Smith as Jack started tapping out the new signal. Then he hurried away.

"I bet he's off to check if the iceberg scratched the paint," joked Jack. "We've probably stopped so he can send down a man with a paintbrush."

Harold laughed so hard he nearly choked on his cake.

This photograph shows Harold Bride in Titanic's radio room. The SOS message tapped out by Jack Phillips was the first ever sent by an ocean liner.

Harold Bride

One of the two radio operators who tapped out calls for help, Harold was forced out of the radio room when water surged in.

SOS

SOS, the Morse code message tapped out by Jack Phillips in *Titanic*'s radio room, is an emergency signal that is recognized throughout the world. *SOS* doesn't stand for *Save Our Souls*, as some people think. It is used simply because its code, *dot dot dot, dash dash dash, dot dot dot* (· · · — — — · · ·), is very easy to remember and send quickly.

In-depth info

To discover more about the objects and scenes that the storytellers encountered on their eventful voyage, click the coloured words.

Consultant: Dr Eric Kentley
Project Editor: Louise Tucker
Project Art Editors: Emma Forge, Tom Forge
Art Director: Bryn Walls
Managing Editor: Miranda Smith
Managing Production Editor: Stephanie Engel
Cover Designer: Neal Cobourne
DTP: John Goldsmid
Photo Editor: Diane Allford-Trotman

Library of Congress Cataloging-in-Publication Data Available
Distributed in the UK by Scholastic UK Ltd, Westfield Road, Southam, Warwickshire, England CV47 0RA

ISBN 978-1-407-13843-5

10 9 8 7 6 5 4 3 2 1   14 15 16 17 18

Printed in Singapore   46
First published 2014

Scholastic is constantly working to lessen the environmental impact of our manufacturing processes. To view our industry-leading paper procurement policy, visit www.scholastic.com/paperpolicy.

"I have never seen anything so magnificent, even in a first-class hotel. I might be living in a palace."
—ARTHUR GEE, FIRST-CLASS PASSENGER

TITANIC'S BOILERS, IN THE HARLAND AND WOLFF SHIPYARD

Contents

Unsinkable giant

Titanic became the largest ship in the world when it was completed in 1912. These workers – dwarfed by the giant propellers of *Titanic*'s near-identical sister ship, *Olympic* – thought, as did many people at the time, that the mighty vessels were the safest ever

Sea and be seen

Titanic had broad decks where passengers – like these second-class guests – could stroll. To avoid spoiling the view, the first-class promenades were kept clear of lifeboats. Although *Titanic* had more lifeboats than the regulations required, there were not enough to carry all the passengers.

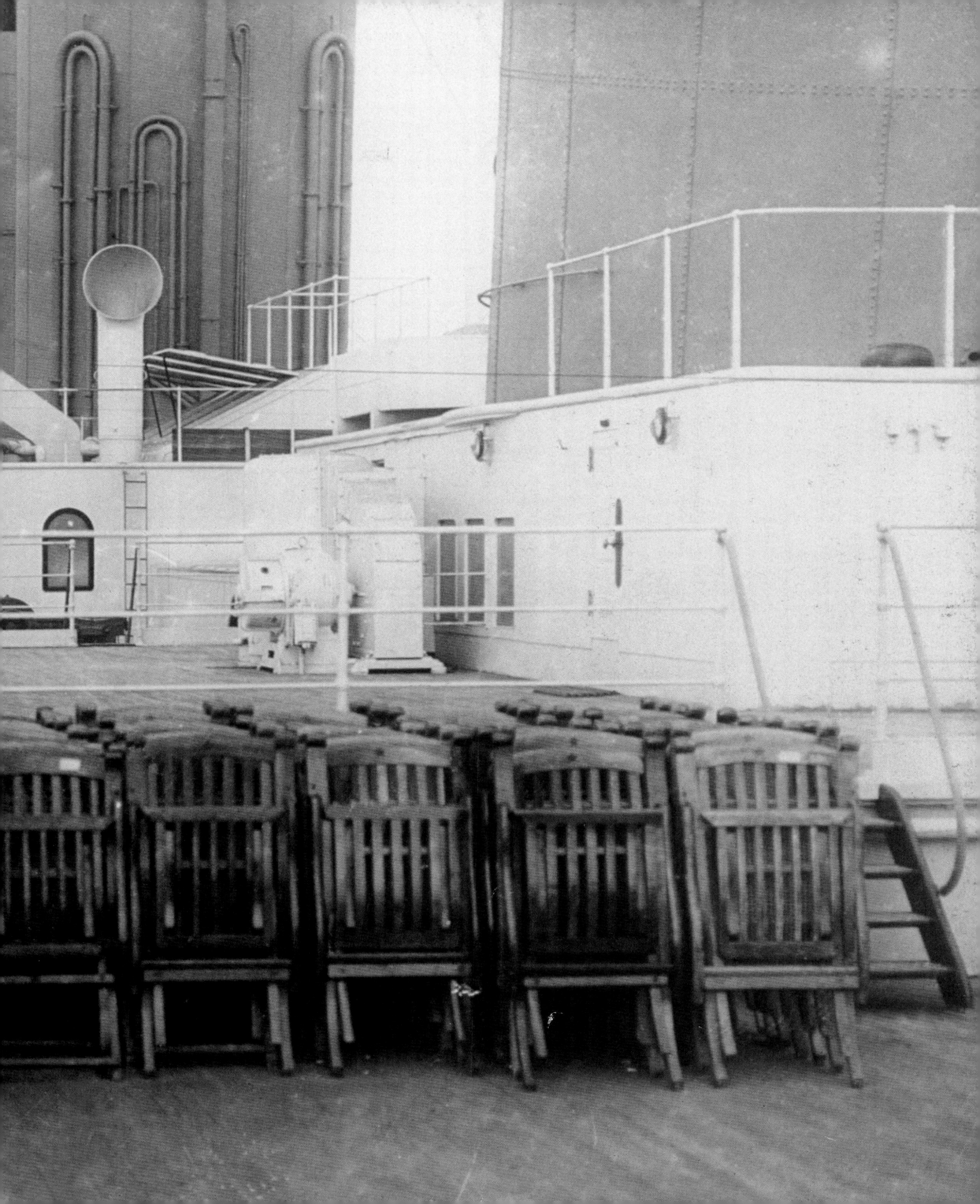

WHITE STAR LINE

Crossi
Atla

* Which shipping lines competed for passengers?

* Where was *Titanic* carrying passengers to?

* What did promenaders do for exercise?

ng the
ntic

The ship of dreams

Titanic was already a famous ship in 1912. Then, four days into its first voyage, it became the world's most famous shipwreck. The tragedy, with its cast of millionaires and immigrants, and the story of the long search for the wreck captivate us to this day.

The *Titanic* legend

Dramatic accounts of *Titanic*'s last moments, and of its heroes and villains, have been retold many times over the years, in many media.

THE BRITISH FILM *A NIGHT TO REMEMBER* (1958)

JAMES CAMERON'S BLOCKBUSTER (1997)

At the movies
Film director James Cameron visited *Titanic*'s wreck on the seabed. For his 1997 film, *Titanic*, Cameron used his footage of the wreck and meticulously re-created the ship and its sinking.

Unsinkable

Titanic was the largest and most luxurious ship in the world. This vast iron and steel construction represented a high point in British manufacturing. It carried the most current technology, such as radio and electrical equipment. And, according to the owners, the watertight doors made it unsinkable.

Maiden voyage
Titanic sailed from Southampton at noon on Wednesday, 10 April 1912. As it pulled away from the shore, its enormous propellers sucked another ship out of its berth. The two ships almost collided, to the alarm of *Titanic*'s passengers.

Titanic]

Arguments

People are still debating the disaster and what caused it. Was it human or mechanical error? Why did *Titanic* sail into an ice field at high speed? Why weren't there enough lifeboats? Why did the ship sink so quickly? Why didn't a nearby ship help? Was it an avoidable tragedy? Read the facts, then decide what to think for yourself.

"I cannot imagine any condition which would cause a ship to founder. I cannot conceive of any vital disaster happening. . . . Modern shipbuilding has gone beyond that."

—*TITANIC*'S CAPTAIN, EDWARD JOHN SMITH, IN 1907, QUOTED BY THE *NEW YORK TIMES* ON 16 APRIL 1912

"The loss of the *Titanic* was due to criminal carelessness in running at full speed through the ice with a new crew, despite the fact that [the captain] had received repeated warnings by wireless of the vast ice field and bergs that lay in his path."

—MAJOR ARTHUR PEUCHEN, FIRST-CLASS PASSENGER, DISCUSSING CAPTAIN SMITH IN AN INTERVIEW WITH THE *TORONTO WORLD* ON 20 APRIL 1912

More here

For key to symbols, see page 112.

Captain Edward John Smith
Carpathia shipwreck
Major Arthur Peuchen

Titanic*: Voices from the Disaster*
by Deborah Hopkinson

882½ Amazing Answers to Your Questions about the **Titanic**
by Hugh Brewster and Laurie Coulter

A Night to Remember (1958) is a well-researched film about the boat and the sinking.

Secrets of the Titanic (1986) is a documentary about finding the wreck.

Titanic (2012), a TV mini-series, follows passengers of different classes on board the ship.

The **Titanic – 12,450 Feet Below** exhibit at **Mystic Aquarium** in Mystic, Connecticut, USA, tells the story of the ship and of the discovery of the wreck.

Visit **Titanic: The Experience** in Orlando, Florida, USA, to tour full-scale re-creations of rooms on the ship and see items from the wreck, including part of the hull.

Story of a disaster

Titanic's story began when rival shipping companies competed to make money by building the biggest and best ship ever. *Titanic* was White Star's ultimate ship, yet it sank in only a few hours. The discovery of the wreck in 1985 added a fascinating new chapter to this tragic story.

1907
Rival lines
Cunard was White Star's main rival for USA-bound European passengers. Cunard launched the sleek, fast liners *Mauretania* and *Lusitania* on the transatlantic route. White Star decided to compete with even bigger ships.

ONE OF *MAURETANIA*'S POWERFUL PROPELLERS

1880
A new start
The Age of Migration began as Europeans escaped famine, poverty, or persecution by moving to the USA. They boarded fast new steamships to cross the Atlantic Ocean.

CHEAP FARES ENCOURAGED MILLIONS OF EUROPEAN EMIGRANTS TO SAIL WEST

1908
Harland and Wolff put up an enormous steel frame over two new slipways to build the liners Olympic and Titanic.

GIANT GANTRY

•1870 •1880 ••1900 •1910

White dots represent 10-year increments.

WHITE STAR LINE

18 JAN. 1868
Businessman Thomas Ismay bought the White Star Line, a shipping company that had gone bankrupt.

1869
Irish shipbuilder Harland and Wolff started making ships for White Star.

JULY 1908
White Star's owners agreed on the design for the new ships that were to be built by Harland and Wolff.

MAR. 1909
Titanic's keel was laid down at Harland and Wolff's yard number 401.

OCT. 1910
Riveters finished attaching the huge steel plates that formed Titanic's hull.

1902
American takeover
US banker J. P. Morgan bought White Star for the International Mercantile Marine Co. He wanted to control the transatlantic travel market so that he could raise prices. He provided funds to build new White Star ships.

J. P. MORGAN
Owner, International Mercantile Marine Co.

Lived   1837–1913

Morgan was a powerful and influential businessman who ran railway and steel companies. He booked a passage on *Titanic* but cancelled at the last minute.

31 MAY 1911
Cheering crowds
Many thousands watched *Titanic* touch water for the first time at its launch. Ten months of finishing and fitting out began, turning it into a floating palace.

TITANIC'S LAUNCH

10 APR. 1912
Setting sail
Titanic departed from Southampton. Its passengers included wealthy people who liked to travel on the maiden voyages of luxury liners.

PASSENGERS BOARDING

16 APR. 1912
Sinking ship
Relatives of *Titanic's* passengers and crew, desperate for news of survivors, besieged White Star offices. The names were slowly radioed from *Carpathia*, and the world was shocked that so many lives had been lost on an "unsinkable" ship.

CROWDS AWAITING *CARPATHIA'S* ARRIVAL

14 APR. 1912
Titanic *sailed into the night at full speed, despite warnings of icebergs on the route.*

11:40 PM, 14 APR. 1912
Titanic *hit an iceberg. Few believed the damage was serious, and lifeboats were launched with empty seats.*

18 APR. 1912
Arriving in New York, Carpathia was met by a crowd of 40,000.

31 MAY 2009
Millvina Dean, the last survivor from Titanic, *died. She had sailed on the ship as a two-month-old baby.*

19 APR.–3 JULY 1912
US and British authorities both held inquiries.

ICEBERG!

1912 / **10** · · · ● · · ● ● · ● · · · **·17** ● **·18** ● **·19** / **·1980** ● ● ● · · **·2010**

White dots represent 1-day increments.

FEB.–APR. 1912
Coal shortages meant that fuel had to be saved for Titanic. So White Star cancelled other voyages and transferred passengers to Titanic.

2:20 AM, 15 APR. 1912
Titanic sank. Only one lifeboat returned for survivors. Others feared the weight of more people would sink them, so they stayed away.

SEPT. 1985
An expedition led by Dr Robert Ballard discovered remains from Titanic scattered across the ocean floor, 3,701 m (12,144 ft) down.

JULY–SEPT. 1987
An expedition recovered about 1,800 objects from the wreck.

4:10 AM, 15 APR. 1912
Rescue ship
The liner *Carpathia* rescued the first boatload of survivors after a freezing night at sea. Many needed treatment for frostbite.

INJURED RADIO OPERATOR HAROLD BRIDE

13 JULY 1986
Wreck explored
The submersible *Alvin* explored and photographed the wreck stuck in the sand. The images sparked fresh interest in *Titanic's* story.

TITANIC'S BOW ON THE SEABED

2,223 people were on *Titanic*; only 706 survived

Ship technology

In the late 19th century, the demand for bigger, faster ships spurred the development of transatlantic liners powered by new technologies such as steam turbines and propellers.

Travel to a new land

Millions of people left Europe for new lives in the United States. The only way to reach the USA was to sail across the Atlantic Ocean – a long journey at the time.

Safe harbour
The large liners could dock only at ports with deep, ice-free harbours.

EUROPE

Hamburg
Liverpool
Southampton

ATLANTIC OCEAN

Boston
New York

NORTH AMERICA

Sleek or wide?
Some ships were designed with sleek hulls, to slice quickly through the water. Others were built in wider, more stable shapes, to fit extra passengers.

HULL SHAPED FOR SPEED

WIDER HULL WITH MORE SPACE

New cabins

Propellers replaced paddles, freeing up space for more cabins. This area became the quarters for "steerage", or third-class, passengers. Fares were low, but they added up to profits for ship owners.

Paddles
Paddles (right) took up a lot of space and required large quantities of coal to power them.

Propellers
The enormous propellers on the new ships provided more

From sailboats to liners

Ships increased in size to carry more passengers and to hold the coal that was needed to power the new steam engines. To be the biggest and best, liners were beautifully furnished, like luxury hotels.

SS Great Western
This oak-hulled boat, powered by a steam-driven paddle, was built for Atlantic trade.

SS Great Western

First voyage	1838
Owner	Great Western Steamship
Propulsion	Paddles and sails
Speed	8.5 knots (16 kph / 10 mph)

16-day crossing

148 passengers

SS Great Britain
This was the first iron ocean liner with a propeller.

SS Great Britain

First voyage	1845
Owner	Great Western Steamship
Propulsion	A propeller and sails
Speed	11 knots (20 kph / 13 mph)

14-day crossing

360 passengers

SS *Teutonic*
This was the first modern liner built especially for passengers.

No more sails
Teutonic was the first White Star liner without sails.

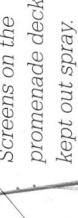

SS *Teutonic*
First voyage	1889
Owner	White Star
Propulsion	Twin propellers
Speed	20 knots (37 kph / 23 mph)

6-day crossing
1,490 passengers

SS *Kaiser*
This was the first four-funnel liner.

SS *Kaiser Wilhelm der Grosse*
First voyage	1897
Owner	Norddeutscher Lloyd
Propulsion	Twin propellers
Speed	22 knots (41 kph / 25 mph)

6-day crossing
1,506 passengers

RMS *Mauretania*
This superfast liner offered luxury accommodation.

RMS *Mauretania*
First voyage	1907
Owner	Cunard
Propulsion	4 propellers
Speed	26 knots (48 kph / 30 mph)

5-day crossing
2,198 passengers

Titanic's twin sister
RMS *Olympic* was built before *Titanic* was. The shipbuilders copied many features from *Mauretania*. These included elevators, a French-style café, and a grand staircase. *Titanic's* design had more first-class cabins.

Safety measure
Watertight compartments helped prevent sinking.

RMS *Olympic*
At the time, this was the world's most luxurious ship.

Deck windows
Screens on the promenade deck kept out spray.

RMS *Titanic*
Titanic was the world's largest ship when it was built.

RMS *Titanic*
First voyage	1912
Owner	White Star
Propulsion	3 propellers
Speed	22.5 knots (42 kph / 26 mph)

6-day crossing
2,223 passengers
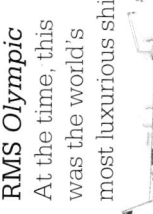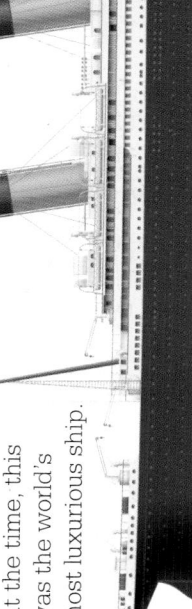

Transatlantic rivals

Shipping companies White Star and Cunard battled for the ticket money of millions, competing to build the best ships. The race inspired the giant, luxurious *Titanic*.

White Star Line

White Star originally took gold seekers to Australia, but it failed when the gold rush faded. Under Thomas Ismay, it turned its attention to the United States.

1845 — The White Star Line was founded in Liverpool.

1868 — White Star went bust and was bought by Thomas Ismay.

1869 — Ismay hired Harland and Wolff shipyard to build all White Star ships.

1876 — The company profited by carrying Royal Mail.

1899 — Thomas Ismay died, and his son J. Bruce Ismay took his place.

1902 — American J. P. Morgan added White Star to his International Mercantile Marine fleet.

1907 — Ismay and Harland and Wolff agreed to build three ships, including *Olympic* and *Titanic*.

WHITE STAR LINE

Luxury liners

With money from US financier J. P. Morgan, J. Bruce Ismay began to develop liners of unparalleled luxury that could compete with Cunard ships. His ships left Southampton for New York every Wednesday.

Why White Star?
Even passengers in third class on a White Star liner were treated well. Families, single women, and married couples were given their own cabins.

Special colours
These ships had "White Star buff" and black funnels.

J. BRUCE ISMAY
Chairman, White Star Line
Lived   1862–1937
Ismay always travelled on his ships' maiden voyages.

[Big shippers]

CUNARD LINER

State of the art
Cunard was the first shipping line to regularly run passenger ships on transatlantic routes. It introduced new technologies such as turbine engines, electricity, and radio. Its ships sailed from Liverpool to New York every Saturday.

Why Cunard?
Cunard's biggest selling-point was the speed of its ships. But it also began to match White Star in comfort.

Red livery
All Cunard ships had red and black funnels.

New rival
German line Norddeutscher Lloyd (NDL) became a major transatlantic rival in 1897. In that year, it launched *Kaiser Wilhelm der Grosse*, which won the Blue Riband for the fastest ocean crossing.

Power of four
NDL's *Kaiser Wilhelm der Grosse* set a trend with its four funnels.

Cunard Line
Cunard was named after its founder, Samuel Cunard. He won a contract to carry British mail across the Atlantic. His line also carried emigrants.

1840 Samuel Cunard founded the British and North American Royal Mail Steam Packet Company.

1848 The growing fleet started making trips to New York.

1880 The fleet was renamed the Cunard Line, and more ships were built.

1881 Cunard's new all-steel liner, *Servia*, was one of the first ships with full electric lighting.

1902 The British government loaned Cunard money for two superliners.

1903 Hungary agreed to send 30,000 emigrants a year to New York on *Carpathia*.

1907 Lusitania joined the fleet, followed by her sister ship *Mauretania*.

SAMUEL CUNARD
Founder, Cunard Line
Lived 1787–1865
Cunard moved from Canada to Britain to run his company.

CUNARD LINE

Promenaders

On a promenade – a long, open walkway – people could relax, chat, and show off their finest clothes. In the early 20th century, it was a place to see and be seen. There were promenades in parks, gardens, and seaside towns, such as this one by the coast in Scarborough, in northeast England. They were so popular that ocean liners provided promenade decks so that passengers could take leisurely strolls.

Immigration [Dream ticket]

Between 1836 and 1914, more than 30 million Europeans sailed across the Atlantic Ocean for a fresh start in the United States. They were often escaping famine, poverty, or persecution. Ocean liners such as *Titanic* were crammed with immigrants.

Rising numbers

The peak of the Age of Migration was in 1907, when 1,285,349 Europeans stepped onto US soil for the first time. By then, 15.7 percent of the US population was made up of people who had been born in other countries.

Promise of work

The United States needed people to make clothes, build homes, and farm the western part of the country, which was becoming accessible by rail. There were many opportunities for workers.

Coming to the USA
Total immigration figures clearly show the overall rise in numbers of immigrants.

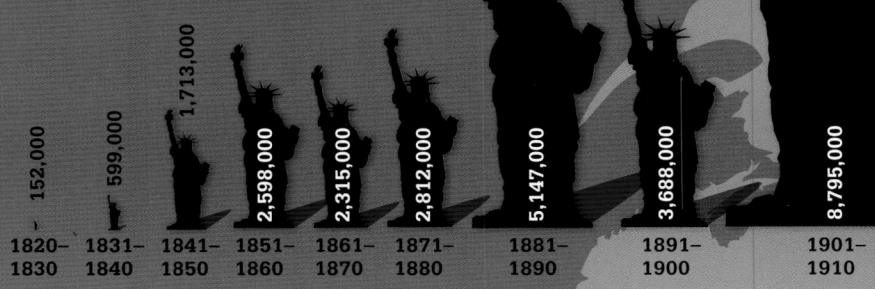

1820–1830	1831–1840	1841–1850	1851–1860	1861–1870	1871–1880	1881–1890	1891–1900	1901–1910
152,000	599,000	1,713,000	2,598,000	2,315,000	2,812,000	5,147,000	3,688,000	8,795,000

UNITED STATES

Ellis Island

70%
of all immigrants entered through New York

Spreading west
Farmland was available to people willing to open up the hostile prairie frontier and grow crops for the increasing population.

High-rise living
Many Europeans went to cities such as Chicago, Philadelphia, and New York, where they crammed into tall tenements.

Eyewitness

NAME: Golda Meir

LIVED: 1898–1978

FROM: Russia

DETAILS: Golda Meir's father left his family in Russia in 1903 to travel to the USA. It took him three years to save the money for his wife and three daughters to join him. Golda was eight then. She later became prime minister of Israel.

❝ I can remember only the hustle and bustle of those last weeks in Pinsk. . . . Going to America then was almost like going to the Moon. . . . We were all bound for places about which we knew nothing at all and for a country that was totally strange to us. ❞

Ellis Island

In 1890, the US federal government took control of the rising number of immigrants. A new facility was built on Ellis Island in New York Bay. Third-class passengers were ferried from their ships to Ellis Island to be checked for illnesses and interviewed. About 2 percent were sent back where they had come from.

Annie Moore

Annie Moore, a 15-year-old from Ireland, and her younger brothers were the first to enter Ellis Island.

Mass exodus

The mass exodus from Europe was triggered by many circumstances. Religious or political persecution, lack of food or shelter, and a desire for land were just some of the reasons people left their homelands for the unknown.

IRELAND

SCANDINAVIA

RUSSIA

GERMANY

EASTERN EUROPE

ITALY

Seeking new land
Most Scandinavian emigrants were rural workers and wanted land to farm.

Crop failure
In 1845, Ireland's potatoes – an essential crop – were devastated by blight, leading to famine.

Poverty
In Germany, new factories lowered pay and raised prices, and land was in short supply.

Prejudice
From 1881, Russian Jews were persecuted and massacred. Millions left.

Eastern European exodus
Poverty and overpopulation caused the Great Economic Immigration from 1880 onwards.

Emigration from Italy
A rising population in Italy meant that there was not enough work available.

Irish emigrants
Around 1.5 million Irish people left for the USA in a single decade, 1845–1855.

famine
persecution
poverty

First steps
On arrival, passengers disembarked, then underwent medical tests. (Those who failed were sent to the hospital.)

Waiting in line
Then they lined up for hours in the registry room and were questioned about how they would support themselves.

The Flag of Faces
Today, four in every ten Americans can trace their ancestors back to the people who passed through Ellis Island.

Iceberg ahead!

Dangers for transatlantic liners included other ships, fog, and ice. Icebergs are hard as rock, sharp as knives, and mostly hidden underwater.

Iceberg Alley

Each spring, powerful currents drag fresh icebergs and sea ice south through a stretch of sea 400 km (250 miles) off the coast of Newfoundland, Canada. The ice moves towards the busy shipping routes of the north Atlantic Ocean, forming an area known as Iceberg Alley.

Collision course
The fatal iceberg glided for more than 1,600 km (1,000 miles) to reach *Titanic*'s path.

Greenland

Iceberg Alley

ATLANTIC OCEAN

Key
Path of iceberg
Titanic's course

How icebergs form

About 100 glaciers along the coast of Greenland produce the majority of the icebergs that float into the north Atlantic Ocean. Roughly 15,000 icebergs form in that area every year. The iceberg that sank *Titanic* began its existence thousands of years ago, as snowflakes falling across Greenland. Over time, the snow became part of a glacier, which moved slowly toward the sea. Finally, a section calved, or broke off, to form the fatal iceberg.

1 Snowing hard
Snow builds up over thousands of years on high ground. It melts in summer and freezes in winter, forming grainy snow called firn. Fresh snowfall presses the firn down to form solid ice.

2 Glacier
Over the following centuries, layers of ice are crushed into a huge, dense block. This forms a glacier, a giant, slow-moving river of ice. The glacier, pushed by its own weight, moves down towards the sea.

[Snow monster]

Hidden danger

About 85 percent of an iceberg lurks underwater, where its sharp edges do the most damage to ships. Even the section above water is almost impossible to see on a dark night.

Shape changer

Melting and winds constantly change the shapes and sizes of icebergs.

Dark matter

Scattered grit and sections of darker ice can make an iceberg hard to see.

4.5 M (15 FT) ABOVE WATER

26 M (85 FT) UNDERWATER

Giant ice cube

Weighing 100,000–200,000 tonnes on average, icebergs float low in water.

3 Calving
When the glacier reaches the coast, huge sections of ice crash into the ocean. This process, calving, can cause huge waves.

4 Underwater mountain
The mountain of ice is so heavy that most of it is hidden underwater. Deep, powerful ocean currents catch the iceberg and sweep it towards the open ocean.

5 Lurking threat
Eventually the iceberg drifts south into warmer waters and begins to melt. But it does not melt away quickly. For a long time, it is still a threat to anything that crosses its path.

Buil
the sh

* Why were *Titanic's* funnels set at an angle?

* How many giant boilers were built for *Titanic*?

* Where on the ship could passengers cycle?

ling
ip

Shipbuilding [Bigger and

The Harland and Wolff site in Belfast, Ireland, was one of the biggest shipyards in the world. Before work could begin on White Star's two new superliners, a gantry, a crane, and two giant slipways had to be built.

Profitable partners

Harland and Wolff had an agreement to design and build all of White Star's ships. Under the contract, the shipbuilder could charge White Star for all the costs of building a ship, plus an extra 5 percent of pure profit.

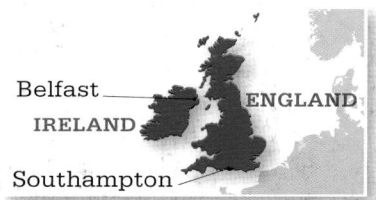

Shipyard and port
Titanic was built in Belfast, Ireland, but sailed for the USA from Southampton, England.

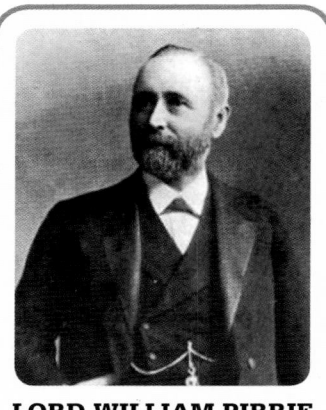

LORD WILLIAM PIRRIE

Chairman, Harland and Wolff

Lived 1847–1924

Pirrie started work at Harland and Wolff in 1862, as a 15-year-old apprentice. He rose through the ranks and began running the company in 1895. He toured the site each day to check that every job was done properly.

Eyewitness

NAME: Bram Stoker

DATE: 1907

FROM: Ireland

DETAILS: The author of *Dracula* visited the Harland and Wolff shipyard in 1907. He called it the world's greatest shipbuilding yard.

“ No sooner is a vessel launched than preparations begin for laying the keel of another. . . . In the doing of this great work . . . all seems simple, whether it be in perfected details or vast combination. The building of a ship appears to be mere child's play. ”

Titanic
The half-built Titanic *remained on the slipway after its sister ship* Olympic *was launched.*

Gantry
This 67-m (220-ft) tall metal framework carried 16 mobile cranes.

On track
Belfast began running electric trams in 1905, thanks to profits from the busy shipyard.

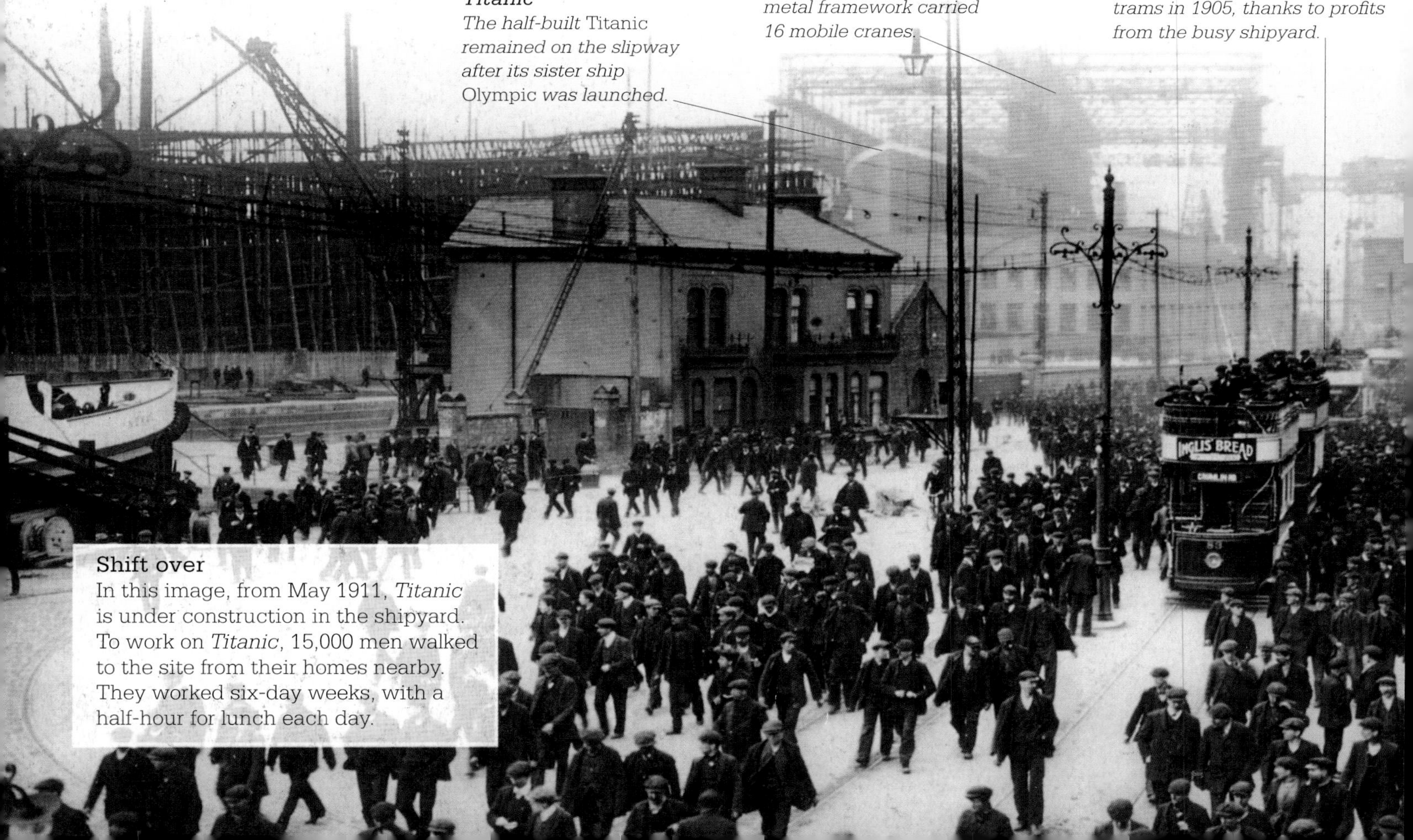

Shift over
In this image, from May 1911, *Titanic* is under construction in the shipyard. To work on *Titanic*, 15,000 men walked to the site from their homes nearby. They worked six-day weeks, with a half-hour for lunch each day.

Floating crane

Fitting *Titanic*'s massive boilers and funnels would have been impossible without this 200-tonne floating crane. It was shipped in from Germany in 1910.

Lifting power

The new crane, 46 m (150 ft) tall, was berthed between the ship and the dock. It was used to fit the 60-tonne, 19-m (62-ft) high double-walled funnels.

Complete job

Nearly every structural part of the two ships, as well as many of their fixtures and fittings, was designed and made on-site.

Latticed steel

Counterweight
This exerted the force needed to lift up to 250 tonnes.

Funnel

Jib
This is the moving arm of the crane.

Hinge
This allowed the jib to tilt.

1 Making it
Harland and Wolff had workshops for every part of a ship, from engines and staircases to beds and funnels.

2 Moving it
Heavy goods were transported around the 121-hectare (300-acre) site by 50 steam-powered cranes on railroad tracks.

3 Fitting it
When a funnel was lifted into place, it was bolted to the deck with a slight backwards tilt – to make the ship look speedy.

Keel to hull [Steel body]

The first step in building the biggest ship in the world was to construct the strongest hull. The keel was the ship's spine, with frames curving up and beams running across. Steel plates covered the structure to create the hull, or outer shell.

Handcrafted

The hull had to be built in stages to make sure the ship was resilient. On 31 March 1909, *Titanic*'s designer laid the first keel plate. Then frames and beams were attached. Finally, plates were fitted onto the frames to form a watertight exterior.

Gantry
Before work began, a gantry, a huge frame, was built to carry workers and equipment.

1 Starting March 1909: keel laid
The keel formed the strong base along the length of the ship. Wooden blocks, laid at a slight incline, held the steel sections of the keel upright as they were joined together.

Keel
The keel was formed from steel beams – 1.3 m (4.3 ft) at their widest points.

Steam crane
A system of cranes, powered by steam, moved heavy parts and equipment.

2 April 1910: framework finished
Workers attached 300 curved steel frames to the keel. The frames supported the beams, which ran across the ship and held up each deck.

Metal "glue"

Titanic's iron rivets were about 2.5 cm (1 in) thick and 7.5 cm (3 in) long. They held the hull's giant plates together.

How a rivet works

A rivet was heated to soften it, pushed through holes in two metal plates, held in place on one side, and hammered flat.

Rivet **Rivet head**

Fitted
A heated rivet fitted through two overlapping hull plates.

Steel plates

Hammered
Striking the rivet clamped the plates together.

Flattened head

Teamwork

Four-person teams used long hammers to beat the rivets. They were paid based on how many rivets they fitted, making this competitive work. A record of 12,000 rivets hammered in 1 week was set in 1909.

Smashing time
When riveters stood on scaffolding and beat rivets into place from both sides of the metal hull, the noise was deafening.

Plates
Steel plates measured at least 2.5 cm (1 in) thick.

3 million rivets
held the ship together

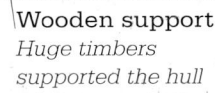

Built for strength
The hull extended 29.5 m (97 ft) in height from the keel to the boat deck.

Framework
Frames were spaced further apart in the middle of the hull, where there was less stress on the ship.

3 October 1910: plating finished
The "skin" of the ship was made up of 2,000 riveted steel plates. The largest plates were 11 m (36 ft) long and 1.8 m (6 ft) wide, and weighed 3.4 tonnes.

Wooden support
Huge timbers supported the hull while it was built.

Mighty hull
The hull covered the biggest ship in the world – 269 m (882.8 ft) long and 28 m (92 ft) wide.

The workforce

A workforce of thousands toiled six days a week for three years to build *Titanic*. It was noisy and dangerous work – 8 men died and 246 were injured.

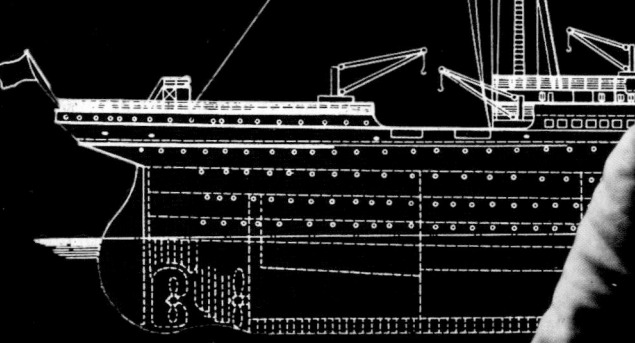

Line by line
Thomas Andrews, *Titanic*'s designer, oversaw the detailed plans for the ship as they were drawn by hand at the shipyard.

Work and school

About 20 percent of the workforce was unskilled labourers. The skilled labourers carried out the many specialized jobs needed to build a luxury liner. They included young apprentices learning trades.

Titanic job list

Blacksmith
Boilermaker
Carpenter
Draughtsman
Electrician
Engineer
Joiner
Painter
Plumber
Riveter
Sheet-metal worker

SKILLED £2
UNSKILLED £1

Payday

Each Friday, workers were paid in cash. The unskilled labourers earned about as much as the ship stewards did.

Thomas Andrews

Like his uncle Lord William Pirrie (see page 30), who ran the shipyard, Andrews regularly walked around the site to note every detail of the work.

THOMAS ANDREWS
Ship designer

Lived	1873–1912

Andrews spent five years learning how to design and build ships at Harland and Wolff. He then became a director at the yard and designed *Titanic*. Andrews headed the guarantee group on *Titanic* – a team of nine shipbuilders who were there to solve problems on the maiden voyage.

Expert skills

Large, light spaces were built for the draughtsmen, who designed and drew up plans. Other specialists included carpenters, who built furniture and ship fittings, and blacksmiths, who forged metalwork.

DRAUGHTSMEN   CARPENTERS   BLACKSMITHS

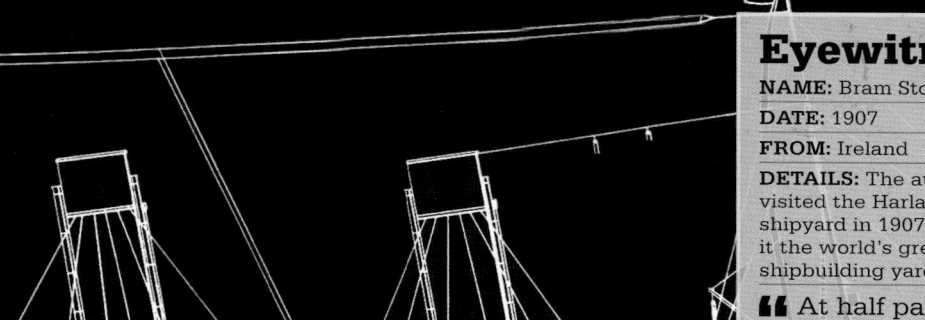

Eyewitness

NAME: Bram Stoker

DATE: 1907

FROM: Ireland

DETAILS: The author of *Dracula* visited the Harland and Wolff shipyard in 1907. He called it the world's greatest shipbuilding yard.

66 At half past five o'clock on Friday afternoon a horn blows, and section by section the men line up outside the score of pay-offices. At twenty minutes to six the last man passes out with his salary. 99

More here

For key to symbols, see page 112.

Edward James Harland
Gustav Wilhelm Wolff
Queen's Island, Belfast

"The Last Rose of Summer" and **"Danny Boy"** are typical of the popular Irish songs that were probably sung at the shipyard.

Visit **Titanic Belfast** in Northern Ireland, built on the slipways where the ship itself was built.

See the People's Story exhibition at the **Ulster Folk & Transport Museum** in Northern Ireland to explore the lives of the people who built *Titanic*.

apprentice: a person learning to do skilled labour.

draughtsman: a person who draws plans of machinery that will be built.

forge: to heat and hammer metal in order to change its shape.

Finest and fines

The very best workers were asked to join the guarantee group, which sailed on maiden voyages. The worst workers faced fines for breaking the many rules, about everything from making tea to stealing.

1 DAY'S PAY — **STEALING TOOLS**

0.5 DAY'S PAY — **BEING LATE**

0.5 DAY'S PAY — **PLAYING SOCCER**

0.25 DAY'S PAY — **MAKING TEA**

0.25 DAY'S PAY — **SMOKING**

Tough bosses

Managers were not afraid to be strict – they could easily replace bad workers with the labourers who lined up each day hoping for work.

Danger at work

Thousands of men carrying equipment along planks high above the hull spelled danger. Men were injured by falling or by being hit by equipment. One worker was crushed to death at the launch.

Casualties
Many workers suffered minor injuries, and eight died.

218 MINOR INJURIES

Deaths and injuries

28 serious injuries

6 building deaths

1 launch death

1 workshop death

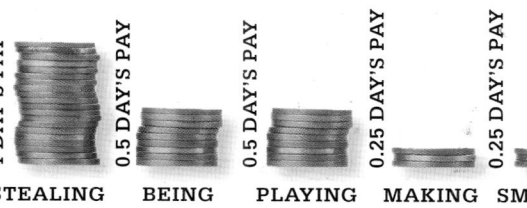

Young and old
The 15,000 workers included boys as young as 14 years old.

Powerhouse

The 29 boilers that were needed to power *Titanic* were built by skilled boilermakers in the Harland and Wolff shipyard. Each boiler was the size of a three-storey house and contained three or six furnaces to burn the coal that heated water flowing through a network of pipes. The steam that was created powered the engines, generated electricity, supplied the refrigeration plant, and heated the ship's public rooms and the second- and third-class cabins.

Fitting out

An army of workers spent ten months transforming *Titanic*'s giant steel hull into a floating palace. Preparations involved everything from laying 320 km (200 miles) of electric cable to screwing in the last brass doorknob.

Rigging
Steel ropes supported the mast and funnels.

Davit
Lifeboats were held by and lowered from steel arms called davits.

Porthole
The glass in the 1,200 portholes was at least 2.5 cm (1 in) thick.

Out of the water
The ship was propped up in a dry dock while the propellers were fitted and the outside painted. Meanwhile, inside the ship, thousands of workers toiled around the clock to equip and furnish *Titanic*.

Timeline: Preparations

April 1911 *Preparations began, with the boilers and engines installed first. For a while, Titanic had just three working funnels in place.*

20 September 1911 *Olympic collided with Royal Navy cruiser Hawke and came to Belfast for repairs. This delayed work on Titanic.*

11 October 1911 *The date of Titanic's maiden voyage, first planned for March 1912, was pushed back to April 1912.*

January 1912 *Sixteen lifeboats were installed on sturdy steel davits on the promenade deck.*

"When the tugs were left behind . . . [*Titanic*] left for Southampton, carrying with her the best wishes of the citizens of Belfast."

—*BELFAST NEWS LETTER*, 3 APRIL 1912

Mainmast
The steel and wood mainmast towered 47 m (154 ft) above A Deck.

Aft crane
The aft cranes primarily loaded food into the refrigerated storerooms.

Paint
A thick coat of oily paint reduced damage from salt water.

3 February 1912 *The ship was moved to dry dock to fit the propellers and paint the hull. Inside, a Marconi radio was installed.*

March 1912 *The sliding windows on the promenade of A Deck were fitted, one of many alterations made after assessing Olympic.*

31 March 1912 *The ship was complete. Decorating continued. Later, flowers hid the smell of new paint.*

2 April 1912 *Five tugs towed Titanic out for sea trials. Later that day, it left Belfast for the overnight trip to Southampton.*

Decks 1–5 [Top class]

The officers and first-class passengers could work or relax on the top five decks, far away from the noise and smell of the engines.

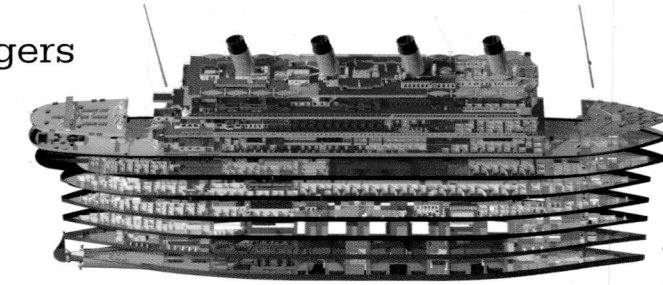

TITANIC'S DECKS

LENGTH: 269 M (882.8 FT)

A place for everyone

All the classes and most of the crew used the top decks, but they rarely crossed one another's paths. Signs, walls, lockable gates, and separate staircases kept them apart. Strict social divisions were maintained.

Café Parisien

Wicker chairs and real ivy plants gave this elegant place the look and feel of a French sidewalk café. It was especially popular with the younger passengers.

Poop deck

Here, third-class travellers could enjoy the views and sea air. Filthy smoke from the funnels drifted over their heads as they walked around the deck.

Elevator
Second-class passengers had their own elevator.

Lifeboats

Docking bridge

Second-class dining saloon
This large, oak-panelled room had a grand piano so that diners could enjoy music with their food.

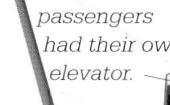

Cranes for loading cargo

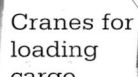

Two bathrooms for third class

Third-class surgery

Surgery
This room above the hospital was where the doctor saw first- and second-class patients.

Hospital
This had 12 beds. Next to it was a ward with 6 beds, to isolate those with infectious diseases.

Gym

Gym goers could "race" each other on cycling machines as a large dial showed their speeds. The man here, Lawrence Beesley (see page 54), was in second class but was allowed to try the gym.

Marconi space

The two Marconi radio operators lived and worked in three rooms: an office, a soundproof room for the noisy transmitter, and a shared cabin.

Grand staircase

This 18-m (60-ft) high, 5-m (16-ft) wide staircase rose up through the five decks and was topped by a large chandelier and a giant glass dome.

First-class lounge

Compass tower

First-class reading and writing room

Officers' quarters
Six officers' cabins were here, with their own promenade outside.

Bridge
This was the command centre for the ship.

BOAT DECK

Crow's nest
Lookouts worked on a platform equipped with a bell and telephone.

Class location

First-class facilities were in the stable middle of the boat, where people were less likely to be seasick.

Less movement in first-class cabins

More movement in third-class cabins

Three first-class elevators

A DECK

FORECASTLE DECK

B DECK

Crew's hospital

C DECK

D DECK

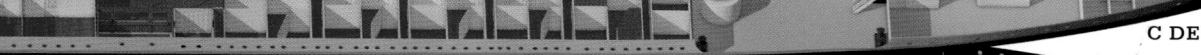

First-class dining saloon
This elegantly decorated room gave more than 500 diners a smooth ride in the centre of the ship.

Staterooms
These first-class rooms had the best views.

Third-class open area
Passengers sat on wooden benches in this area.

Deck names
Some decks had traditional names. For example, the boat deck got its name because lifeboats were stored there.

Decks 6–10 [Powerhouse]

The lower decks housed the workers and the engines that ran the ship. Lower-class passengers and cargo were fitted in around them.

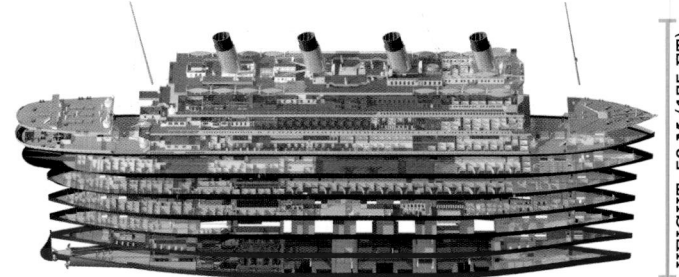

HEIGHT: 53 M (175 FT)
Boat layout
First class
Second class
Third class
Crew
Storage
***TITANIC*'S DECKS**

Lowest levels

Titanic's lowest row of portholes was on G Deck, just above the waterline. Below was the hot, noisy, and dirty underworld that powered the ship.

Engines

On each side of the ship, an engine ran a propeller. Steam from the engines also ran a central propeller and a turbine. This produced a smooth, efficient journey.

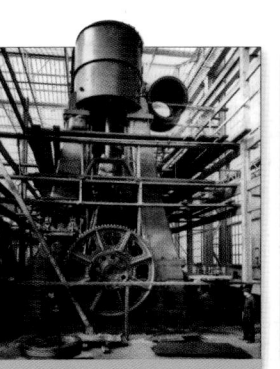

Barber shop

The second-class barbers sold toys, souvenirs, postcards, and pens with the *Titanic* and White Star logos – plus pincushions shaped like life jackets.

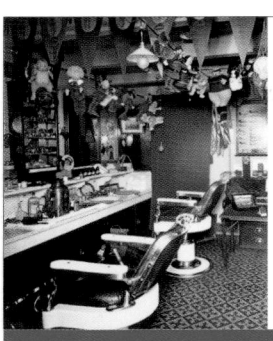

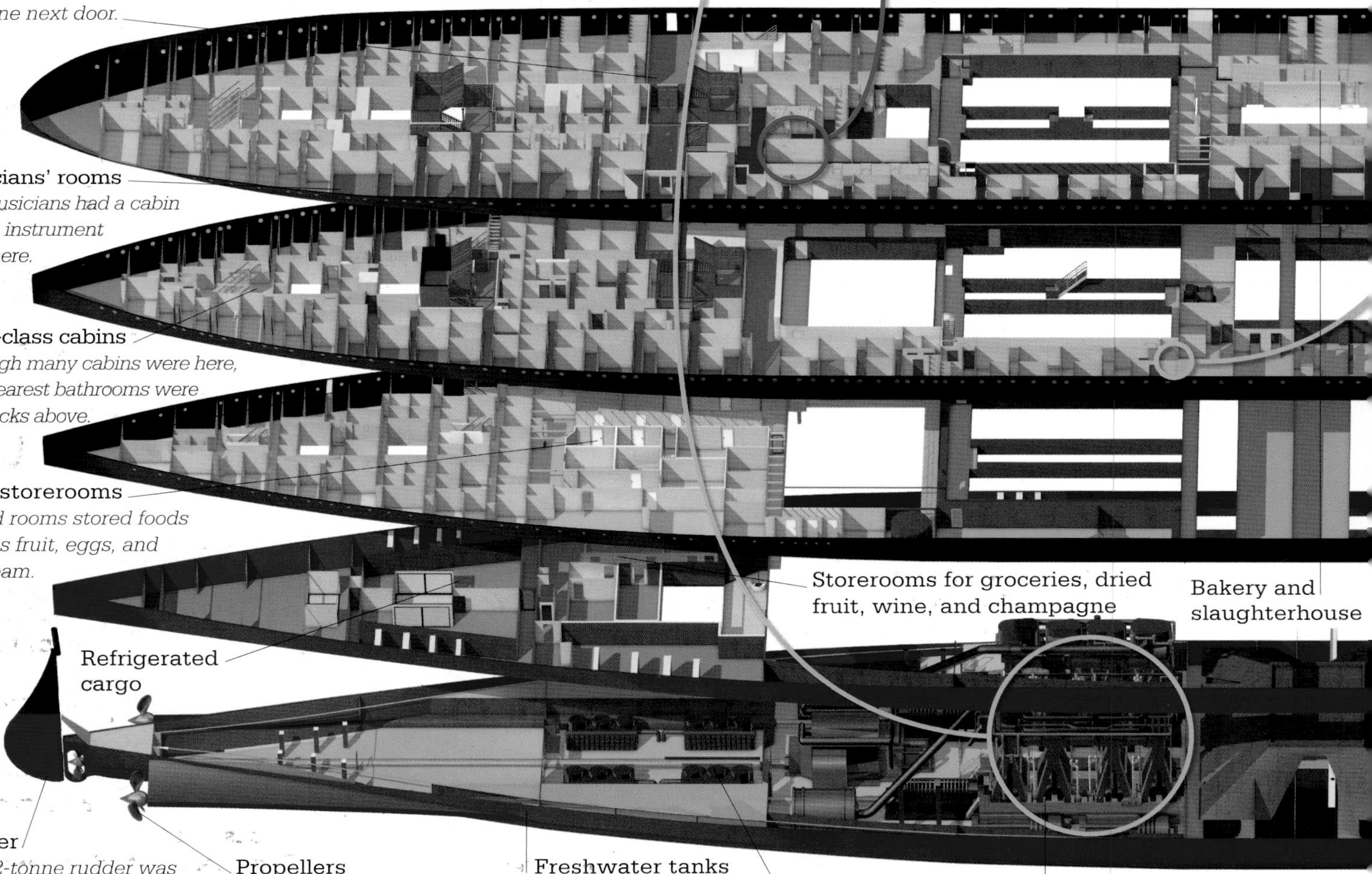
Potato storage
This held 36 tonnes of potatoes, and there was an electric peeling machine next door.
Musicians' rooms
The musicians had a cabin and an instrument room here.
Third-class cabins
Although many cabins were here, their nearest bathrooms were two decks above.
Food storerooms
Chilled rooms stored foods such as fruit, eggs, and ice cream.
Storerooms for groceries, dried fruit, wine, and champagne
Bakery and slaughterhouse
Refrigerated cargo
Rudder
The 92-tonne rudder was 24 m (79 ft) high and 5 m (15 ft) wide. Seven massive pivoting bolts held it in place.
Propellers
Each outer propeller measured 7 m (23 ft) across and weighed 34.5 tonnes.
Freshwater tanks
Seven tanks like these held a total of 873 tonnes of drinking water.
Electricity supply
Electricity was generated by four dynamos.
Engine rooms
The two main engines were as tall as a three-storey house.

Kennels

Titanic had its own dog kennels. The fare was £2 per animal, plus a butcher's fee for meat scraps. The crew exercised dogs on the poop deck. White Star was also happy to carry cats, birds, and monkeys.

Turkish baths
Visitors to the Turkish baths relaxed in heated steam rooms, then plunged into a cold pool. This was followed by massages called shampoos. The walls were lined with blue and green tiles.

Swimming pool
Titanic was one of the first liners with a pool. It was filled with heated seawater and was popular with passengers, although the water sloshed around as the ship rolled.

Scotland Road
This passageway was named after a busy street in the port of Liverpool.

Waiters' cabins

Stewards' bathrooms

Shared cabins
These were cheap, sparse cabins for single men.

E DECK

Third-class dining room

F DECK

Squash court

G DECK

Post office

Specie room
Gold and silver coins were secure here, hidden behind luggage.

ORLOP DECK

Ballast tank

TANK TOP

Boiler rooms
There were 24 double-ended boilers and 5 single-ended boilers.

Double bottom
The tank top formed the double bottom of the hull, a safety feature.

Orlop deck
The orlop deck was not a solid deck – it was a platform that the engines rose through.

Decks 6–10
Passengers went only as low as G Deck. Cargo space and the tank top, where the ship's engineers and firemen worked, lay below.

Safety [Unsinkable?]

Was *Titanic* safe? It included all the most modern safety features. Crew, passengers, and bystanders alike were convinced that the ship was unsinkable.

Radio for help

Titanic was equipped with a new technology – wireless radio. This had already helped another ship in peril. On 23 January 1909, RMS *Republic* struck another ship and began to sink. Radio distress signals summoned other vessels and lifeboats to ferry 1,700 people to safety.

Cork float panels
Cork panels enabled life jackets to float for at least 24 hours.

Radio headset
Headsets like this warned the crew of dangers ahead, such as ice fields.

Plenty of life jackets
Titanic stored 3,560 cork and canvas life jackets all over the ship, in wardrobes and on racks. They did not need to be inflated.

Eyewitness

NAME: Captain John Ranson

DATE: January 1909

FROM: United Kingdom

DETAILS: John Ranson was an experienced captain who commanded White Star ships for many years. He was captain of *Baltic*, one of the ships that heard *Republic*'s distress calls and came to its aid.

“ Who would have thought ten years ago of wireless messages to be used in saving life at sea? . . . The passenger on a well-equipped transatlantic liner is safer than he can be anywhere else in the world. ”

Eyewitness

NAME: Charlotte Collyer

DATE: 10 June 1912

FROM: Basingstoke, UK

DETAILS: Charlotte Collyer boarded *Titanic* with her husband and daughter. Like many others, she thought *Titanic* was the safest of ships.

“ There is one impression that will never leave me. It is the irony of the faith that I had in the big ship. 'She is unsinkable,' I had been told. 'She is the safest boat afloat.' ”

Unsinkable

White Star's promotional materials highlighted the ship's safety: "These two wonderful vessels [*Olympic* and *Titanic*] are designed to be unsinkable."

Eyewitness

NAME: Karl Behr

DATE: c. 1912

FROM: New York

DETAILS: Karl Behr was a 26-year-old US tennis star who went to Europe and boarded *Titanic* to follow the woman he wanted to marry.

" To our minds the idea of the *Titanic* sinking was preposterous. . . . We had read about many of the features of this great new ship, of which not the least emphasized was its unsinkability. "

Eyewitness

NAME: *New York Times*

DATE: October 1910

FROM: United States

DETAILS: The *New York Times* ran an article on *Olympic*, *Titanic*'s sister ship. The paper was impressed by the ship's safety features.

" So complete will be the system of safeguarding devices on board this latest of ocean giants that . . . it is claimed that she will be practically unsinkable and absolutely unburnable. "

More than enough lifeboats

Board of Trade regulations said that ships that weighed more than 9,000 tonnes – *Titanic* was 46,328 tonnes – should carry 16 lifeboats. *Titanic* had 20.

Lifeboats
Titanic carried 16 wooden boats and 4 canvas "collapsibles."

Eyewitness

NAME: Sir Alfred Chalmers

DATE: 1912

FROM: British Board of Trade

DETAILS: Sir Alfred Chalmers was nautical adviser to the British Board of Trade from 1896 to 1911. He decided that large liners did not need more lifeboats, because they were so safe. At the British inquiry after *Titanic*'s sinking, he explained his reasoning.

" I found [that ships were] the safest mode of travel in the world. . . . [16 lifeboats] was the maximum number that could be rapidly dealt with at sea and that could be safely housed. . . . If you went on crowding the ships with boats you would require a crew . . . which would be carried uselessly across the ocean, that never would be required to man the boats. "

Safely secured
A jacket was put on over the head and secured with fabric ties.

Watertight compartments

There were 15 watertight doors that could be closed from the bridge of the ship. These created 16 watertight compartments along the bottom half of the ship. The ship could stay afloat even if 4 of these compartments flooded.

Laura Mabel Francatelli's life jacket
This canvas life jacket belonged to one of *Titanic*'s survivors, Laura Mabel Francatelli, who was 30 years old at the time of the sinking. She was secretary to Lady Duff Gordon (see pages 50–51) and came from London. The life jacket carries her faded signature as well as the signatures of seven other survivors.

Eyewitness

NAME: Unnamed journalist

DATE: June 1911

FROM: *Shipbuilder* magazine

DETAILS: This magazine ran stories about how ships were made. In 1911, it devoted a whole issue to *Titanic* and its sister ship *Olympic*, including this description of the watertight compartments.

" In the event of an accident, or at any time when it may be considered advisable, [the] captain can, simply by moving an electric switch, instantly close the emergency doors . . . and make the vessel practically unsinkable. "

The Voy

* Who added glamour at Cherbourg?

* What new invention was carried as cargo?

* How was the grand staircase lit up?

age

Setting off [All aboard]

On the morning of Wednesday, 10 April 1912, passengers boarded the towering *Titanic* for its maiden voyage. At Southampton, the new crew struggled to direct people to their cabins, through a maze of corridors filled with vases of flowers to disguise the smell of fresh paint.

Welcome to *Titanic*

First-class passengers were welcomed aboard by officers or the captain. Those in third class had quick medical inspections to make sure that they were healthy and would be allowed into the United States.

Boarding ports

CHERBOURG: 274

SOUTHAMPTON: 958

Queenstown: 123

Passengers on and off
Passengers could board at several ports, and some did not travel all the way to the US. At Cherbourg, France, 24 people got off *Titanic*, and 7 left at Queenstown, Ireland.

First-class view
From the moment passengers arrived to board *Titanic*, they were divided by their ticket class. First-class passengers boarded at the highest level, and third class at the lowest gangway.

Eyewitness

NAME: Charles Lightoller

LIVED: 1874–1952

FROM: Hampshire, UK

DETAILS: Lightoller was second officer on *Titanic*. He was going to be first officer but was replaced by William Murdoch, who was transferred to *Titanic* at the last minute.

❝ At last sailing day arrived, and from end to end the ship, which for days had been like a nest of bees, now resembled a hive about to swarm. As 'zero' hour drew near, so order could be seen arriving out of chaos. On the stroke of the hour, the gangway was lowered, the whistle blew, ropes were let go, and the tugs took the strain. ❞

First-class service
There were two special boat trains from London to Southampton. One was reserved for first-class passengers, who were escorted by White Star staff.

IRELAND

Queenstown
Irish emigrants boarded here.

3 ## Queenstown

ENGLAND

Boat trains from London

London

Next stop:
New York

1

Southampton

Southampton
This harbour was deepened to accommodate large liners.

First ports of call
Titanic crossed to France and Ireland for more passengers and mail before heading west.

Cherbourg
Americans returning from Europe and Africa boarded at this port.

2 ## Cherbourg

FRANCE

Last stop
At Queenstown, a fleet of boats ferried sellers of Irish lace, linen, and woollens to *Titanic*. American millionaire John Jacob Astor IV bought plenty of finery from the vendors for his new wife, Madeleine.

Margaret Brown
Brown was a wealthy American who had met the Astors on their honeymoon in Egypt. When Brown heard that her grandson was very ill, she decided to travel home with the famous couple, and they boarded at Cherbourg.

First class [Millionaire style]

For passengers in first class, *Titanic* was a luxurious hotel run by an army of stewards. First-class cabins were in the stable middle of the ship, where passengers were less likely to be seasick.

The rich list

There were many millionaires on board, as well as other aristocratic and wealthy first-class passengers. Some were travelling on business. Many rich Americans were returning home from vacations in Europe.

1 member of staff served 1.5 first-class passengers

Service

There were 225 stewards to serve 329 first-class passengers. They were on call all day until late evening.

Keeping fit

Instructor Thomas McCawley loved to show off his gym.

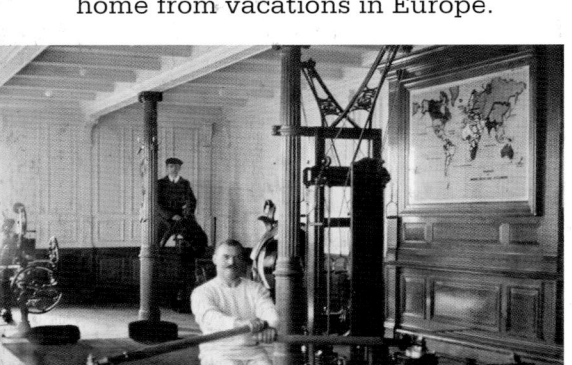

Electricity

Several first-class luxuries were powered by electricity. Most people did not have electricity at home at this time.

Electric steam bath

The electric bath, a box heated by lamps, was a fashionable way to relax.

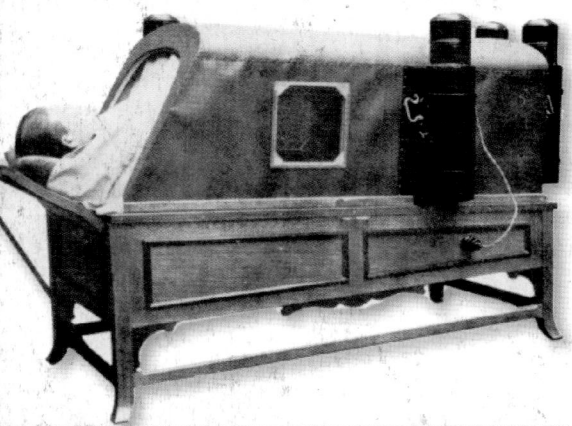

First-class couple

Sir Cosmo Duff Gordon, a member of the British aristocracy, was a Scottish landowner and sportsman who had fenced at the 1908 Olympics. He was travelling with his wife, Lucy.

Electrical luxuries

Heaters
Table fans
Telephones
Dimmable lamps
Hot running water
Doorbells

Cabins

The cabins ranged from comfortable single berths to magnificent parlour suites (see pages 52–53).

Louis XVI stateroom

Among the luxurious fittings were silk wall panels, a stained-glass window, and a chaise longue.

Cabin contents

Wood sprung bed with hair mattress
Chaise longue
Wardrobe
Dressing-table
Washbasin
Carpeted floor

Eyewitness

NAME: Lucy Christiana, Lady Duff Gordon

LIVED: 1863–1935

FROM: London, UK

DETAILS: Lady Duff Gordon was an upmarket dress designer with salons in London, Paris, and New York.

> Like everyone else I was entranced by the beauty of the liner. I had never dreamed of sailing in such luxury. . . . My pretty little cabin, with its electric heater and pink curtains, delighted me, so that it was a pleasure to go to bed. Everything about this lovely ship reassured me.

First-class facilities

Deck areas: promenade deck, plus two private promenades

Lounge

Reading and writing room (for ladies only)

Smoking room (for gentlemen only)

Gymnasium and squash court

Turkish bath and heated swimming pool

Dining room, à la carte restaurant, and two cafés

Barbershop

Grand staircase and three elevators

Cost of most expensive suite: £870 (equivalent to £78,300 today)

The smoking room

A real fireplace, leather chairs, stained-glass windows, and wood-panelled walls inlaid with mother-of-pearl made the first-class smoking room – for gentlemen only – the grandest room on the liner. This picture is of the smoking room on *Titanic*'s sister ship *Olympic*.

Eyewitness

NAME: Ida Straus

LIVED: 1849–1912

FROM: Germany; Straus's family emigrated to the USA when she was five.

DETAILS: Straus was married to Isidor Straus, one of the owners of Macy's department store in New York. They were returning to the USA from a European vacation and were transferred to *Titanic* after their trip on another ship was cancelled due to a coal strike.

❝ What a ship! So huge and so magnificently appointed. Our rooms are furnished in the best of taste and most luxuriously, and they are really rooms, not cabins. **❞**

First-class berths

The design of each first-class cabin was chosen from 11 different historical eras. This stateroom, Cabin B-59, had dark oak panels and a canopy bed in the "Ol Dutch" style. The doors led to the fami rooms in the suite.

Two stateroom suites
These came with private areas on the promenade deck.

Cabin B-59

Glass bars to spread heat

Heater
First-class cabins and bathrooms had electric heaters.

First-class passenger
American Benjamin Guggenheim boarded the ship at Cherbourg with his valet, Victor Giglio, and a friend, Léontine Aubart. He and Giglio were in stateroom B-84. His chauffeur, René Pernot, travelled in second class.

Second class

Second class on *Titanic* was as good as first class on most other liners. Passengers had their own staircase, though it was less grand than the one for first class.

Eyewitness

NAME: Lawrence Beesley

LIVED: 1877–1967

FROM: London, UK

DETAILS: Beesley was a science teacher visiting his brother in Canada.

❝ The ship is like a palace. There is an uninterrupted deck run of 150 m (165 yards) for exercise and a ripping [great] swimming-bath. . . . My cabin is ripping, hot and cold water and a very comfy-looking bed and plenty of room. ❞

"Loto" and "Louis"
These young French boys were rarely far from their father (see page 104).

In the middle

Second-class passengers included teachers, priests, families, servants, and a band of eight musicians. Also among them was Joseph Laroche, the only black passenger on the liner.

Reading encouraged
Children could enjoy books borrowed from the second-class library on C Deck.

Service

There were 76 stewards on hand to serve the 285 second-class passengers. Among their jobs was changing bed sheets every day.

Library steward
One steward was in charge of the second-class library.

1 member of staff served 3.75
second-class passengers

Cabins

These were comfortable, but the beds were attached to the walls, and the floors were tiled, not carpeted.

Bunking up
Many second-class cabins had space-saving bunk beds.

Cabin contents

Beds
Full set of linen
Wardrobe
Small settee
Washbasin
Chamber pot
Single lightbulb, no shade
Linoleum-tiled floor

Stuart Collett
Sidney Clarence Stuart Collett was a 25-year-old student training to be a minister like his father. He had paid £10 10s (equivalent to £945 today) to emigrate and join the rest of his family in New York State.

best?]

Second-class facilities

Deck area: boat deck	
Dining room for shared meals	
Smoking room	
Library (lounge)	
Barbershop	
Shared bedrooms	
Staircase	
Elevator	
Cost of average fare:	*£13*
(equivalent to £1,170 today)	

Eyewitness

NAME: Eva Hart

LIVED: 1905–1996

FROM: London, UK

DETAILS: Hart was seven years old when her family emigrated to Canada. Their first voyage was cancelled because of a coal strike, so they switched to *Titanic*.

❝ My father was delighted when they offered him a second-class passage in the *Titanic*. The whole world was talking about the *Titanic*. . . . I was seven, I had never seen a ship before. . . . It looked very big. . . . My father was so excited about it and my mother was so upset. ❞

Well read and well fed
The second-class library was also known as the lounge. It served as a sitting area where passengers took afternoon tea at 4 PM.

Third class [Better fare]

For many third-class passengers, a ticket on *Titanic* provided much better accommodation than they were used to at home. But they were kept away from first-class areas.

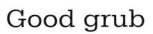

Third-class general room
This large room allowed groups of third-class passengers to gather and chat, sing, dance, or play games. Nearby was a smoking room with a bar for the men to use.

Third-class travellers
Many were families or single men fleeing from persecution or poverty in their homelands. They trekked for many weeks to reach Southampton from eastern Europe or Scandinavia. *Titanic* was the next stage in a journey to a new life.

Good grub
The food provided was basic, but healthy and plentiful. It included porridge, beef with gravy, and stewed fruit.

Food for all
Third-class passengers were served three meals a day in two separate sittings. Women and children also got chicken broth or beef tea at 11 AM – possibly to help fight seasickness.

Dining hall
Long tables were bolted to the floor to keep them from sliding.

Crockery
Plates and cups were plain white with the White Star logo.

Cabins
Cabins for women and families were towards the back of the boat. Single men were at the front.

Four-berth cabin
Most cabins had four or six berths.

Cabin contents
Bunk beds (wood or iron)
Mattresses, pillows, and blankets (no sheets)
Hooks for hanging clothes
Washbasins (some cabins only)

Service
There were 51 stewards, including an interpreter to communicate with the many non-English speakers.

Worldly goods
For many, everything they owned was on the ship.

1 member of staff served 14
third-class passengers

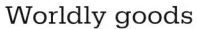

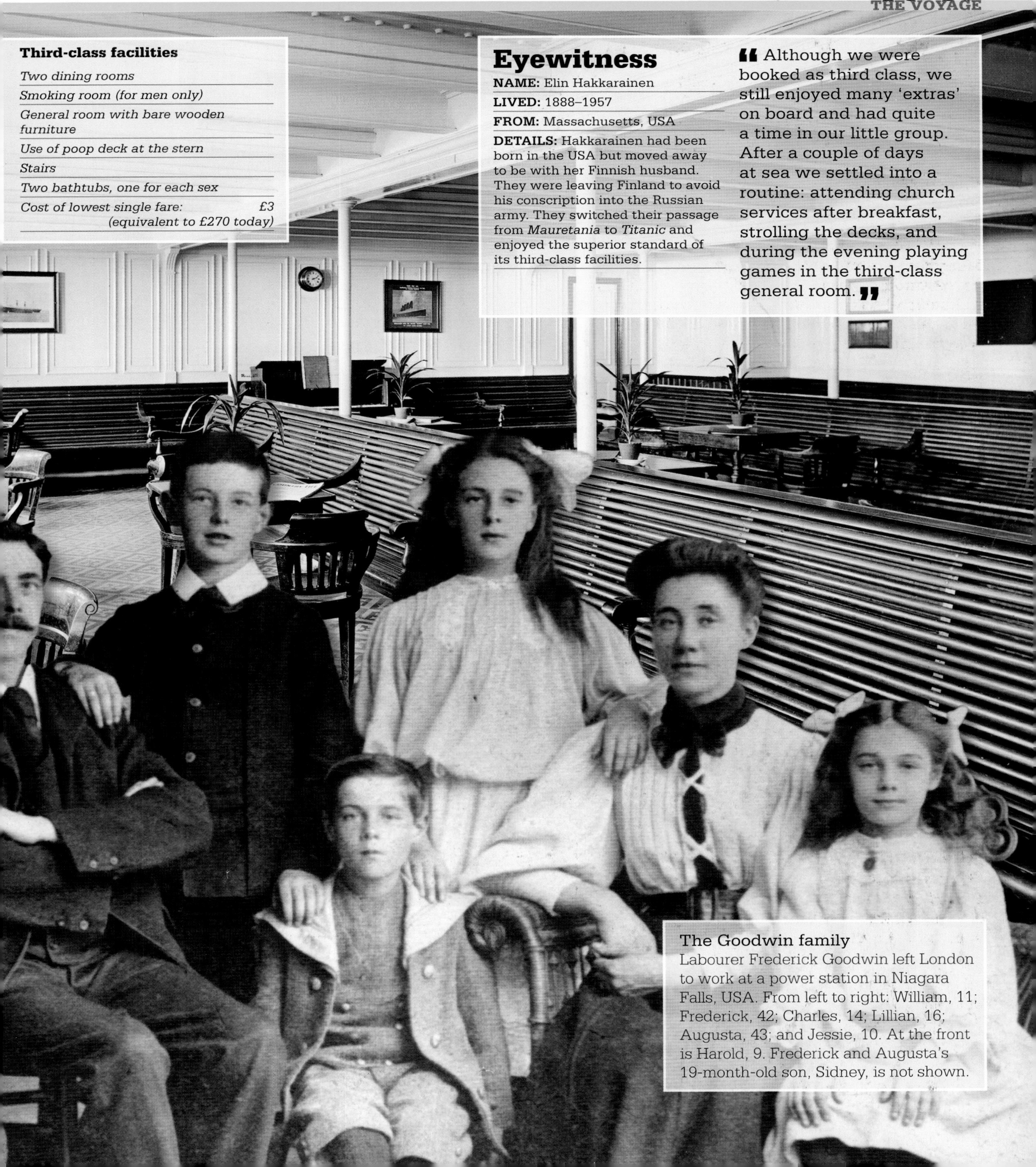

Third-class facilities

Two dining rooms

Smoking room (for men only)

General room with bare wooden furniture

Use of poop deck at the stern

Stairs

Two bathtubs, one for each sex

Cost of lowest single fare: £3
(equivalent to £270 today)

Eyewitness

NAME: Elin Hakkarainen

LIVED: 1888–1957

FROM: Massachusetts, USA

DETAILS: Hakkarainen had been born in the USA but moved away to be with her Finnish husband. They were leaving Finland to avoid his conscription into the Russian army. They switched their passage from *Mauretania* to *Titanic* and enjoyed the superior standard of its third-class facilities.

❝ Although we were booked as third class, we still enjoyed many 'extras' on board and had quite a time in our little group. After a couple of days at sea we settled into a routine: attending church services after breakfast, strolling the decks, and during the evening playing games in the third-class general room. ❞

The Goodwin family

Labourer Frederick Goodwin left London to work at a power station in Niagara Falls, USA. From left to right: William, 11; Frederick, 42; Charles, 14; Lillian, 16; Augusta, 43; and Jessie, 10. At the front is Harold, 9. Frederick and Augusta's 19-month-old son, Sidney, is not shown.

Deck to deck

A walk down *Titanic*'s many staircases took passengers and crew from cool first-class luxury to plain third-class rooms to volcano-like heat from furnaces in the ship's depths.

Many layers

This artist's impression shows how *Titanic* was put together like a ten-layer jigsaw puzzle. The corridors and cabins fitted neatly around big spaces such as the grand staircase, the dining rooms, and the swimming pool.

Letting in the light

During the day, the grand staircase was illuminated by a huge glass dome that allowed the Sun's rays to flow down many storeys. The oval dome was 8 m (26 ft) across. The chandelier in its centre had 50 lights that lit the staircase in the evenings.

Mail room

There were five postal clerks in the mail room. At 48, John Starr March was the oldest of the three American clerks.

Chart room
Here, officers calculated where the ship was and how far it had travelled.

Smoking room
First-class men enjoyed their cigars here.

Enquiry office
Passengers came here to send messages and report problems.

Print room
The crew printed daily menus and news for the passengers.

Third-class bakery
This was one of two bakeries on Titanic that made bread and pastries.

Swimming pool
Men could use the pool 6–9 AM and 2–7 PM. Women could use it 9 AM–2 PM.

Post office
Mail was taken here to be sorted. Then it was stored in mailbags to await arrival in New York.

Watertight compartment

Double hull

Linking and lighting

Two massive staircases, plus many smaller flights, linked the decks, allowing everyone to move around easily. It took 10,000 lightbulbs to light all the rooms, from the tiniest storeroom to the most palatial dining room.

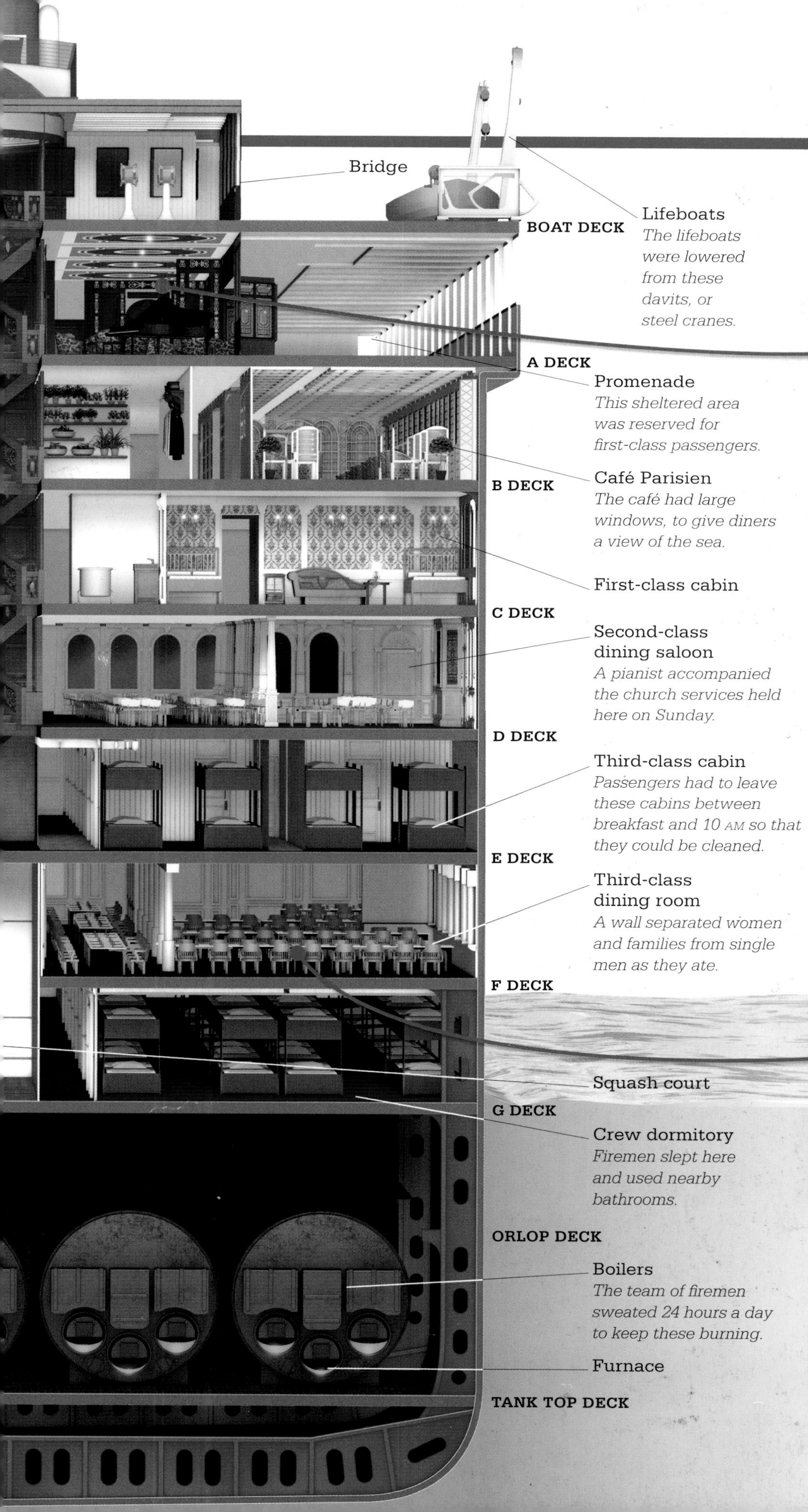

Bridge

Lifeboats
*The lifeboats
were lowered
from these
davits, or
steel cranes.*

BOAT DECK

A DECK

Promenade
*This sheltered area
was reserved for
first-class passengers.*

B DECK

Café Parisien
*The café had large
windows, to give diners
a view of the sea.*

First-class cabin

C DECK

Second-class
dining saloon
*A pianist accompanied
the church services held
here on Sunday.*

D DECK

Third-class cabin
*Passengers had to leave
these cabins between
breakfast and 10 AM so that
they could be cleaned.*

E DECK

Third-class
dining room
*A wall separated women
and families from single
men as they ate.*

F DECK

Squash court

G DECK

Crew dormitory
*Firemen slept here
and used nearby
bathrooms.*

ORLOP DECK

Boilers
*The team of firemen
sweated 24 hours a day
to keep these burning.*

Furnace

TANK TOP DECK

Fine dining
This exclusive restaurant was
open from 8 AM to 11 PM. It
served first-class diners such
as John Jacob Astor IV, the
richest man in the US, and his
wife Madeleine (above).

Eyewitness
NAME: Eileen Lenox-Conyngham

LIVED: 1900–1993

FROM: Edinburgh, Scotland

DETAILS: At age 11, Eileen sailed
on *Titanic* as far as Cherbourg, France.
She, together with her mother, aunt,
and younger brother Denis left the
ship there.

**❝ We were absolutely
staggered by the beauty
and size of this great ship. . . .
The pride of [the] White
Star Line was elegant
beyond description. ❞**

Third class
Jack Prideaux, age 24, was
a steward to *Titanic*'s third-
class passengers. Serving
third class was not a
steward's favourite job – he
was less likely to get tips
from the poorer passengers.

Crew [Many hands]

Titanic's 899 crew members were ranked in a social order, just like the passengers. Officers were at the top, and stewards were in the middle. At the bottom, both in rank and in location, working in the furnaces, were the stokers.

In command

The job of commanding the ship was reserved for the captain and the chief, first, and second officers. Junior officers navigated, marked the ship's charts, and checked air and water temperatures.

New ranks
Henry Wilde joined *Titanic* as chief officer at the last minute. Each of the other officers had to move down a rank.

Harold Lowe
Fifth officer

Hugh McElroy
Chief purser

James Moody
Sixth officer

Charles Lightoller
Second officer

Henry Wilde
Chief officer

Herbert Pitman
Third officer

Edward Smith
Captain

William Murdoch
First officer

Joseph Boxhall
Fourth officer

Popular captain
Officers liked Edward Smith, and wealthy passengers chose to sail on his ships.

EDWARD JOHN SMITH	
Captain	
Lived	1850–1912

Smith left school when he was 13 years old to go to sea; he joined White Star in 1880 as a junior officer. Known as "E.J.", he became the world's highest-paid seaman. Starting in 1904, he commanded all White Star maiden voyages. Smith had planned to retire after his trip on *Titanic*.

Working for tips

Stewards made sure that all the passengers were comfortable: they served food and drinks and cleaned rooms. Stewards hoped for tips to add to their weekly pay of £1 – equivalent to £90 today.

Only 56 of the 899 crew members were sailors

Chief purser
Hugh McElroy was in charge of the stewards and ran the enquiry office. Only the captain and the chief purser dined regularly with the passengers.

A variety of work

There were many jobs on the ship, including specialized radio and postal work. Some crew members were employed by other companies and were regarded as rivals for tips or envied for the privileges they enjoyed.

Musicians
Eight independent musicians played in restaurants and public areas and slept in second class.

Postal clerks
Five postal clerks sorted *Titanic*'s mail freight for the US or British mail services.

Cooks
Luigi Gatti's 66 staff members ran the à la carte dining for first class.

Radio men
Two radio operators, employees of Marconi, sent messages for passengers.

Machine men

Engineers, stokers, trimmers, and greasers kept the ship's machinery running. The men worked in teams, in shifts of four hours on, eight hours off. The members of each team shared a dormitory so that they did not disturb others when they finished their shifts.

Eyewitness

NAME: George Kemish
LIVED: 1888–1912
FROM: Southampton, UK
DETAILS: Kemish, known as "Scooch", earned £6 a month – equivalent to £540 today – to stoke the furnaces. Stokers enjoyed *Titanic*'s new, cleaner conditions.

❝ Being a new ship on her maiden voyage . . . she was a good job in the stokeholds (not what we were accustomed to in other old ships – slogging our guts out and nearly roasted with the heat). ❞

Black gang
Workers in the black gang had the filthy job of fetching and shovelling black coal in the hot, noisy furnaces.

Cargo [Loading up]

When *Titanic* reached Ireland, it collected the last of its passengers. It was also loaded with mailbags. Then it finally set out across the Atlantic towards the United States.

Boarding and landing
The ship was too big for the harbour in Queenstown, so the passengers were ferried out. A new delivery of 194 mailbags was taken to the mail room. There, more than 3,000 bags of mail and 700 packages were already stacked.

Food mountain
The ship had to carry enough supplies for 17 days. There was enough food for the 7,000 meals served daily to passengers and crew.

APPLES: 36,000

FLOUR: 200 BARRELS

ASPARAGUS: 800 BUNDLES

Fresh supplies

Fresh meat	34,000 kg (75,000 lbs)
Butter	2,700 kg (6,000 lbs)
Eggs	40,000
Sugar	4,500 kg (10,000 lbs)
Oranges	36,000
Grapes	450 kg (1,000 lbs)
Lettuce	7,000 heads
Peas	1 tonne
Tomatoes	2.5 tonnes
Potatoes	36 tonnes

Titanic carried
1,665 litres (440 gallons)
of ice cream

Steaming!
Titanic carried 5,345 tonnes of coal, stored in bunkers near the bottom of the ship. A small army of workers called trimmers wheeled and shovelled up to 750 tonnes every 24 hours to fire the 29 boilers.

COAL

Titanic carried
5,000 kg (11,000 lbs)
of fresh fish

Thirsty work
In addition to tankfuls of freshwater, *Titanic* carried 6,800 litres of fresh milk and 20,000 bottles of beer.

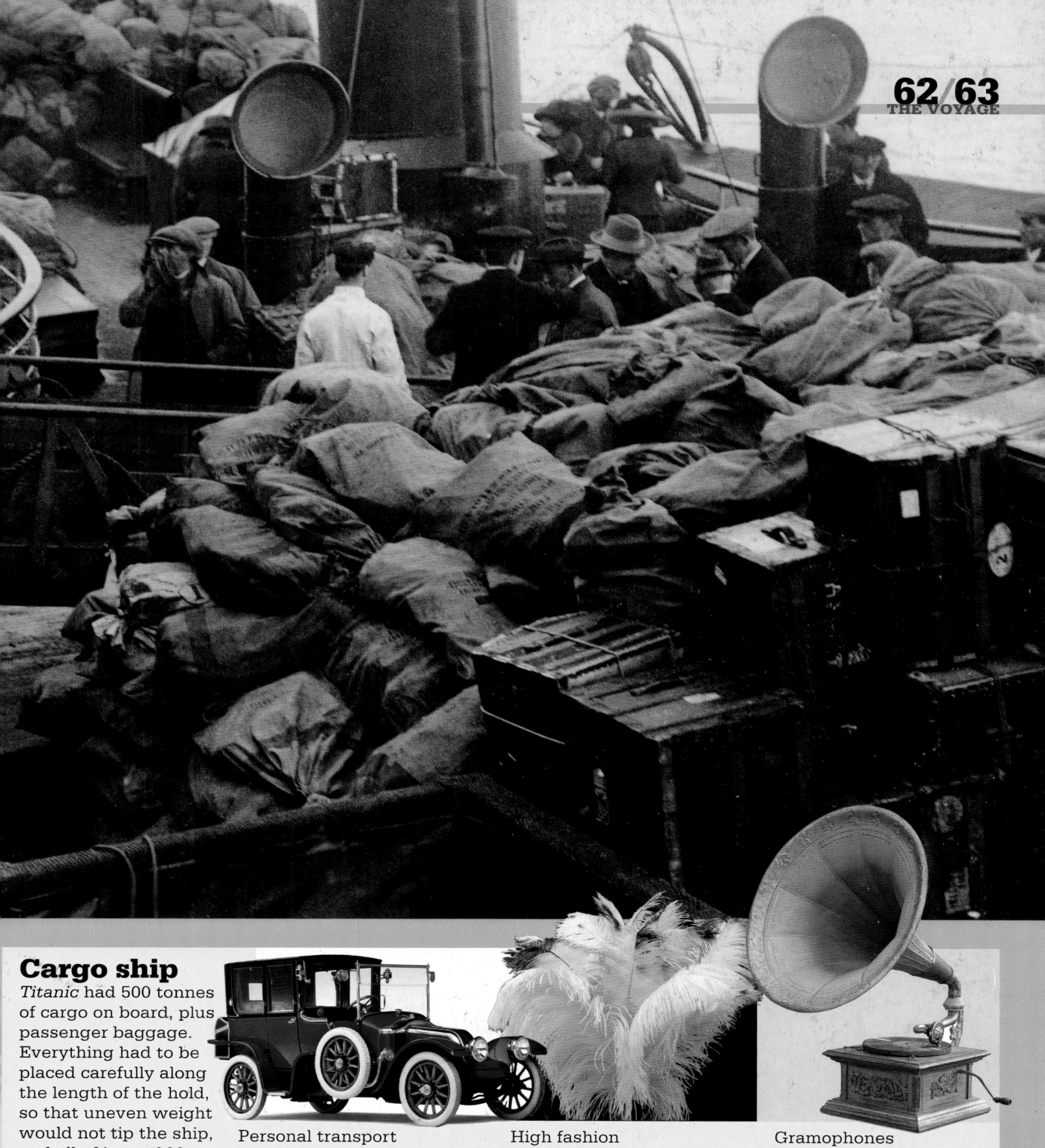

Cargo ship

Titanic had 500 tonnes of cargo on board, plus passenger baggage. Everything had to be placed carefully along the length of the hold, so that uneven weight would not tip the ship, and all of it would be kept secure and dry.

Personal transport
Passenger William Carter brought a Renault car on board in a wooden crate.

High fashion
Titanic carried 12 cases of ostrich feathers, for adding to fashionable clothes in the USA.

Gramophones
A case of some of the newest music players, called Edison gramophones, was on board.

A day on *Titanic*

Titanic was full of activity from early morning until midnight. The crew worked 24 hours a day to serve passengers and sail the ship. Passengers of different classes could not share activities except by special invitation.

Busy days

Passengers were given schedules of mealtimes and other activities. First-class passengers had the most options, but everyone was told when to go to bed.

First class

Second class

Third class

Crew's day

Most crew members worked for four hours, then rested for eight. Stewards were on call nearly all the time. Waiters worked before, during, and after each meal, so a waiter in first class would be on duty for breakfast from 7 to 11 AM.

Shared shifts

The purser and the captain worked the same shifts that most of the crew did.

Wish you were here

Everyone could send letters home. Radio messages, called marconigrams, were charged by the word, and about 60 were sent per day.

Titanic postcard. Postcards of the ship could be bought and mailed to friends back home.

Rooms

Each class had public rooms where passengers could relax. They ranged from very basic to luxurious.

First-class lounge

Along with this comfortable lounge, first class had a smoking room for men and a writing room for women.

Second-class lounge

Also known as the library, this room was mainly for women. Men were more likely to use the smoking room.

Third-class general room

This room and the men's smoking room next door had plain wooden benches and chairs without fabric, so they were easy to clean. Both were for third-class passengers.

The captain toured the ship at 10:30 every morning

[Hours of fun]

New position

Before lunch, officers posted charts to show where *Titanic* had sailed in the past 24 hours. They were proud of how fast the ship could sail.

12:00 PM

How far? Each day's distance was a subject of discussion.

Food

All passengers ate high-quality food, but first class had a choice of restaurants.

Top class

First class had two dining rooms, plus cafés. Elegant dishes included caviar and éclairs.

8–10 AM	Breakfast
1–2:30 PM	Lunch
4 PM	Tea
7–9 PM	Formal dinner

Call to dine
A bugler played at lunch and dinner.

PLATE OF OYSTERS

Come and eat

A gong announced mealtimes. Three-course dinners included a choice of main course, such as curry or fish.

8–10 AM	Breakfast
12:30 PM	Lunch
4 PM	Tea
6:30 PM	Dinner

Dinner plates
Champagne glasses
Oyster forks
Sugar tongs

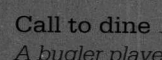

12,000 2,500 1,000 400

***Titanic* tableware**
Plates had different designs in each class. First class were decorated in gold, second's in blue and white, and third's with the White Star logo.

Healthy food

The last three-course meal, eaten at 1 PM on 14 April, was soup, fresh bread, roast beef, and dessert.

Broth snack

Chicken broth and beef tea may have helped ease seasickness.

8–9 AM	Breakfast
11 AM	Broth for women and children
1 PM	Dinner
6 PM	Tea

Special cups
Titanic *had 3,000 broth cups with its company logo.*

Entertainment

Each class had a section of deck to stroll along. Activities on *Titanic* ranged from deck games to music.

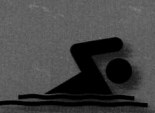
SWIMMING

CYCLING

SQUASH

Sports

First-class passengers could swim, play squash, or use the fitness room.

Tunes

Passengers could listen to the band or play a piano.

GRAND PIANO

Good night!

Lights in the public rooms were switched off to tell passengers to go to bed.

Read, write, or play?

Second-class passengers could stroll on the deck or spend the journey reading, writing, or playing games.

On deck

Deck games such as shuffleboard and quoits were popular.

Lounge

The lounge had a library, and tables for card games.

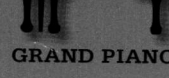

Quoits
Players threw rope rings at a target.

Library
The library even had its own steward.

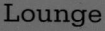

Noisy neighbours

The music and dancing in third class could get very noisy – it sometimes disturbed people trying to sleep in nearby cabins.

Variety show
Passengers played their own small instruments, like this accordion, which were easily carried and stored.

Child's play

Titanic was a giant playground for children, with deck games such as shuffleboard, and a swing on A Deck. Here, six-year-old Douglas Spedden tries out a spinning top on the first-class promenade, watched by his father, Frederic. The Speddens were travelling back to New York after a family holiday in Europe. They survived the sinking, as did Douglas' nanny, Elizabeth Burns.

Navigation [Where are we?]

Today's satellite technology makes it easy to know where you are when you are at sea. But *Titanic*'s crew members had to use tools such as compasses and sextants, and books of complicated tables of the positions of the stars. They relied on lookouts and radio messages to warn them about obstacles.

Latitude and longitude

A ship's location was fixed, or determined, by finding its latitude and longitude. At least two officers, working as a team, took fixes in the mornings and evenings. Between fixes, they used a system called dead reckoning: they estimated the position of the ship based on its speed and direction.

Lines of latitude
These lines show distance north or south of the Equator.

Lines of longitude
These lines show distance east or west of an imaginary north–south line called the prime meridian.

Radio warnings
Radio messages received through these wires warned of icebergs.

Crow's nest
From here, a lookout kept watch for ice ahead.

Navigator
An officer standing on the deck needed sharp eyesight to read a sextant accurately in dim light.

Navigation tools

In order to determine latitude and longitude, speed, and direction, *Titanic*'s navigators needed certain tools. They used a sextant to fix their position, a taffrail log to check speed, a compass to determine direction, and a chronometer to establish longitude. When they had gathered all this information, officers could plot the ship's course on a chart.

Keeping track
The crew plotted the direction of travel on charts.

Rotator
This was towed through the water, turning to match the ship's speed.

Taffrail log
A rotator (top) was attached by a long, stiff line to a reading unit (above) and towed through the water from the stern. The distance

Reading unit
This was usually attached to the taffrail, the rail at

Compass
Titanic's iron hull affected its magnetic field, so its four compasses were mounted on non-magnetic materials such as wood and brass.

Navigating through ice fields

Large ice fields were not a danger often faced by ships on *Titanic*'s route. Ships radioed warnings to one another if they spotted ice, and lookouts scanned the horizon for icebergs. If it was surrounded by icebergs, a ship might stop for the night.

Keeping watch

To spot ice, a team of six lookouts, two at a time, looked for reflected light, dark shapes, and the white foam of waves breaking on icebergs.

BINOCULARS

? What went wrong?

Could *Titanic* have avoided the iceberg? Experts disagree. What do you think? The lookouts' binoculars had been misplaced. But it was a dark, almost moonless night, so it was difficult to see, and the sea was calm, so no waves broke against the iceberg.

"Anyone with experience of ice at sea knows that those very conditions . . . only rendered the detection of icebergs all the more difficult."

—OFFICER CHARLES LIGHTOLLER, IN A BBC INTERVIEW, 1936

"We could have seen [the iceberg] a bit sooner."

—LOOKOUT FREDERICK FLEET, AT THE US INQUIRY, STATING WHAT MIGHT HAVE HAPPENED IF HE HAD HAD BINOCULARS

Ice warnings sent by other ships did not warn *Titanic*'s officers of ice directly ahead, so the ship continued to sail at high speed.

Sextant

A sextant was used to measure the angle between the Sun, or certain stars, and the horizon. Taking a reading allowed officers to draw a position line along which the ship was travelling. Repeating this three times gave them an accurate position.

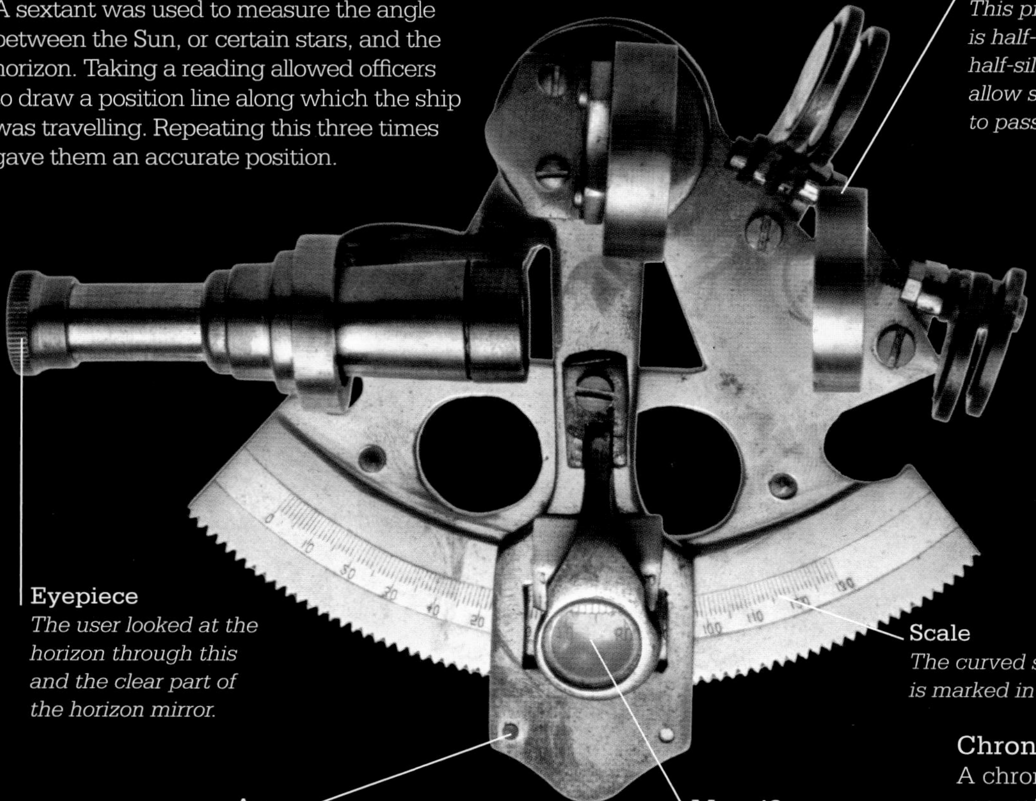

Horizon mirror
This piece of glass is half-clear and half-silvered, to allow some light to pass through.

Local time
The time recorded was compared to the time in, for example, London.

Eyepiece
The user looked at the horizon through this and the clear part of the horizon mirror.

Arm
This was moved until the Sun or a certain star appeared to just touch the horizon.

Magnifier
A magnifying glass helped the navigator read the scale.

Scale
The curved scale is marked in degrees.

Chronometer
A chronometer is a very accurate timepiece. Navigators used it to help determine their longitude. Ordinary clocks, which do not work accurately in extreme conditions, would be affected by the rolling of a ship.

Countdown to disaster

On the fourth day, *Titanic* reached her fastest speed so far. Ahead lay an ice field 125 km (78 miles) wide, so other ships slowed or stopped, and they radioed warnings. But *Titanic* roared into the night on Sunday, 14 April.

12 NOON
Ship's position
Officers used a sextant to determine *Titanic*'s position. They found that the ship had travelled 880 km (546 miles) in 24 hours, at an average speed of 22.06 knots (40.1 kph / 25.4 mph) – its best day yet.

7 PM
High speed
Three boilers, lit that morning, were connected to the engines, which now worked at full power.

BOILERS FIRED UP

5 AM
Up all night
Marconi operators Jack Phillips and Harold Bride finished repairing *Titanic*'s radio. The all-night repairs had left them exhausted, but they started tapping out the huge pile of waiting messages.

A TYPICAL RADIO ROOM

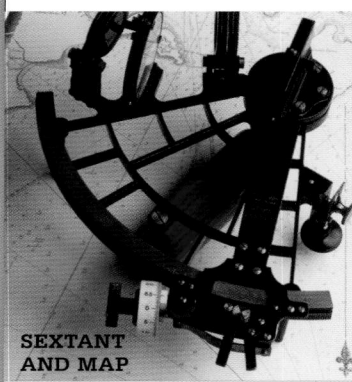

SEXTANT AND MAP

5:50 PM
The ship changed course to be in line for New York.

Timeline

● **5 AM** ○ ● **8 AM** ● ● **11 AM** ● ⚠ ● ● ● ⚠ ● ● **2 PM** ● **5 PM** ● ●

White dots represent 3-hour increments.

9:12 AM
An ice warning was received from Caronia.

11:40 AM
An ice warning was received from Noordam.

1:49 PM
An ice warning was received from Amerika but not sent to the officers on the bridge.

1:54 PM
An ice warning from Baltic was given to Captain Smith, who later handed it to Bruce Ismay.

6 PM
Ismay showed the ice warning to two women as he chatted with them.

Sunday morning
Lifeboat drill cancelled
Captain Smith cancelled a lifeboat drill – nobody is sure why. This meant that the launch of two lifeboats in Southampton was the only time the crew had practised the complicated procedure.

LIFEBOATS ON DECK

1 PM
Early arrival?
Throughout lunch, excited passengers speculated about whether the speeding *Titanic* would reach New York on Tuesday night rather than Wednesday morning.

APRIL 1912						
S	M	T	W	T	F	S
	1	2	3	4	5	6
7	8	9	10	11	12	13
14	15	16	17	18	19	20
21	22	23	24	25	26	27
28	29	30				

[Too fast]

Eyewitness

NAME: Charlotte Collyer

LIVED: 1880–1914

FROM: Basingstoke, UK

DETAILS: Collyer was travelling second class with her husband and daughter. After dinner on Sunday evening, a stewardess warned her that there could be icebergs ahead. Collyer recalled the stewardess's words:

> ❝ '[This] is a dangerous part of the ocean. Many accidents have happened near [here]. . . . Icebergs drift down as far as this.' ❞

10 PM
Missing
New officers started their shifts, and lookouts Frederick Fleet and Reginald Lee climbed up to the crow's nest. They did not have binoculars – these had been misplaced.

11:40 PM
Collision
Lookout Fleet rang the brass bell three times and yelled down the telephone: "Iceberg right ahead." The ship turned hard to starboard to try to avoid it, but 37 seconds later, *Titanic* struck a giant iceberg.

7:30 PM
Officers made careful observations of the stars to pinpoint the ship's position.

Sextant

9:25 PM
Captain Smith went to his cabin.

9:30 PM
Officer Lightoller telephoned the lookouts to remind them to keep a sharp eye out for ice.

11:30 PM
Cyril Evans, the only radio operator on Californian, switched off for the night.

11:35 PM
Titanic thundered along at 22.5 knots (42 kph / 26 mph), its fastest speed so far.

•8 PM · ·11 PM· **11:40 PM**

7:22 PM
An ice warning was received from Californian, which had stopped.

7:37 PM
Titanic was so close to Californian that its radio overheard an ice warning sent to another ship.

8:55 PM
Captain Smith left the dining room and talked with Lightoller on the bridge.

9:52 PM
Mesaba warned of icebergs and pack ice. Jack Phillips did not send the message to the bridge.

11:07 PM
An ice warning from Californian boomed into Phillips' headphones. Busy and annoyed, he tapped out, "Shut up! Shut up!" He did not tell the bridge.

7:10 PM
Ice warning noted
Captain Smith received *Baltic*'s warning telegram back from Ismay so that it could be noted in the chart room.

CAPTAIN SMITH

Eyewitness

NAME: Charles Lightoller

LIVED: 1874–1952

FROM: Hampshire, UK

DETAILS: Second Officer Lightoller later said that if he had seen *Mesaba*'s message, the disaster might not have happened.

> ❝ Without a shadow of doubt, I should have slowed her down at once . . . and sent for the captain. More than likely, . . . he would have stopped the ship altogether and waited for daylight to feel his way through. ❞

BRUCE ISMAY

SU

* How did the crew escape the flooded rooms?

* What hit the seabed first?

* Whose dog took a place in a lifeboat?

Ice monster
This may be the very iceberg that *Titanic* struck. The ship hit the iceberg at 11:40 PM. At the time, nearly all the passengers were asleep, so they did not realize what had happened. But some woke as chunks of ice crashed onto the deck, and others woke when they heard the iceberg scraping the side of the ship. Minutes later, an eerie silence fell on *Titanic* – its engines had stopped.

For up to an hour after *Titanic* hit the iceberg, most of the passengers had no idea how much danger they were in. Below them, stokers (firemen) fought a flood.

Making jokes
Relaxed passengers joked that Captain Smith wanted to repaint the damaged hull before sailing on!

Noisy steam
Escaping steam was so loud that people had to shout to be heard.

Hull damage
The iceberg scraped and bumped along a 90-m (300-ft) stretch of the hull, leaving a series of gashes through which water poured.

Fatal flaw
Titanic's watertight compartments were actually open at the top, so water flowed from one compartment to the next.

Confusion on deck
At 12:05, Captain Smith ordered the crew to prepare the lifeboats. Since Smith had cancelled lifeboat practice, some of the crew did not know where to go or what to do.

Eyewitness
NAME: Eva Hart
LIVED: 1905–1996
FROM: London, UK
DETAILS: Hart's father wrapped seven-year-old Eva in a blanket and carried her to the boat deck.

❝ [My father] said: 'They are going to launch the boats. Purely a precaution; you will all be back on board for breakfast.' . . . He put my mother and I in a lifeboat and he didn't make any attempt to get in himself. ❞

Smoke and steam
After the collision, the engines were shut down immediately. Steam had to be released from the boilers so that they did not explode. The steam was fed into pipes on the sides of the funnels.

Why didn't passengers get in lifeboats?
- Not everyone knew the way to the boat deck.
- It was freezing, noisy, and confusing on deck.
- Many third-class passengers spoke no English.
- Passengers felt safer on *Titanic* than in lifeboats.
- There were no loudspeakers to make announcements.

Lifeboat prep
It took about 20 minutes per boat to remove the cover, plug the hole that let out rainwater, and arrange the ropes to swing the boat out over the ocean.

SCENE FROM THE MOVIE *TITANIC* (1997)

Time line: First hour

11:40 *Laughing passengers kicked and threw chunks of ice that had broken off the iceberg and landed on the decks.*

11:41 *The ship was still and silent for the first time on the trip. Soon after, the boilers started to let off steam noisily.*

11:55 *Mail clerks waded through knee-high water to rescue floating mailbags, hauling them up to the sorting room.*

12:15 *The band played, to try to keep passengers calm. This might have led some to think that the situation was less serious than it was.*

Rockets launched
Distress rockets soared high into the sky, where they exploded into white stars.

Waterway
Rivets burst and water flowed between the plates of the hull.

Hissing pipes
These warned the crew that air was being pushed out by incoming water.

Weighed down
The weight of the incoming water pulled the front of the ship down.

No hope
Once the fifth compartment flooded, nothing could stop water from filling the whole boat.

Eyewitness

NAME: Frederick Barrett
BORN: 1884
FROM: Southampton, UK
DETAILS: Barrett was the leading stoker for boiler room 6. He was standing in the coal bunker when the iceberg opened up a steel plate in it. Barrett scrambled up a ladder over the watertight doorway as it closed, returning minutes later to try to rescue his trapped workmates.

❝ Water came pouring in 0.6 m (2 ft) above the stokehold plate; the ship's side was torn. . . . We did go back, but we could not go in there because there were about 2.4 m (8 ft) of water. ❞

Lifesavers

As the compartments flooded, the crew had to climb emergency ladders to escape, because the watertight doors were locked.

SCENE FROM THE MOVIE
A NIGHT TO REMEMBER (1958)

Radio rescue attempt

At 12:15, Captain Smith asked senior radio operator Jack Phillips to start sending distress messages. Harold Bride helped Phillips as he pounded the transmitter.

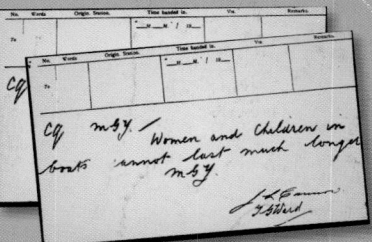

Marconigrams
Any messages received were handwritten on special forms.

12:25 DISTRESS MESSAGE FROM *TITANIC*:

"We have collision with iceberg. Sinking. Can hear nothing for noise of steam."

PHILLIPS TAPPED OUT THIS MESSAGE MORE THAN 15 TIMES IN A ROW, SHOWING HIS INCREASING PANIC.

12:25 *Thomas Andrews told Captain Smith it was possible that Titanic could sink in less than two hours.*

12:30 *The crew loaded women and children onto Lifeboat 7. Many preferred to stay on deck rather than swing out over the sea.*

12:45 *The first lifeboat – less than half full – began its jolting journey 18 m (60 ft) down towards the dark water.*

12:45 *An exploding distress rocket alerted passengers to the fact that the ship truly was in great danger.*

As lifeboats were lowered and the waters rose, people on *Titanic* realized that not all of them would be saved.

Pray with me
Father Thomas Byles said prayers with passengers at the aft end of the boat deck at 2:10.

Last chance
At 2 AM, four men played their last hand of cards at their usual table.

Wake up!
Stewards banged on locked cabin doors to wake passengers who were still asleep. Some in first class had trouble fitting life jackets over their fur coats. Many in third class struggled to haul their belongings along corridors and up stairs.

Bow down
The bow slipped under the waves at 2:17 AM. Behind it, the crew struggled to launch the last two collapsible lifeboats.

First in, first out
First-class passengers had cabins near the top of the ship, so they were closer to the lifeboats stored on the highest deck.

Lifeboats
The crew strictly enforced the practice that, in case of emergency, women and children should be evacuated first. Officers did allow a few men to climb in, and others jumped in as boats were winched down.

Lifeboat launch timeline
The number of passengers on each lifeboat is shown in the red area of the boat.

Lucky Lady
Margaret Hays was travelling first class with two old schoolfriends. She had her tiny Pomeranian dog, Lady, with her. Hays wrapped Lady in blankets and carried her as they boarded Lifeboat 7, the first to be launched. Lady was one of only three dogs that survived.

A POMERANIAN

Eyewitness
NAME: Ida Straus
LIVED: 1849–1912
FROM: Germany
DETAILS: Straus and her husband could have joined her maid on Lifeboat 8, but her husband would not leave with women and children still on *Titanic*.

❝ I will not be separated from my husband. As we have lived, so will we die together. ❞

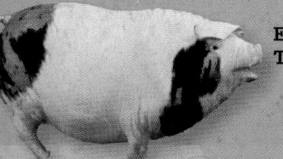

EDITH'S TOY PIG

Heavy landing
A man jumped in, landed on Annie Stengel, and broke her ribs.

Dog on board
This boat included Henry Harper with his wife, servant, and Pekingese dog.

Female driver
English aristocrat the Countess of Rothes steered this boat.

Payload
This was the boat on which Sir Cosmo Duff Gordon paid the crew (see page 97).

28	41	32	25	12
12:45 AM: LIFEBOAT 7	12:55 AM: LIFEBOAT 5	12:55 AM: LIFEBOAT 3	1 AM: LIFEBOAT 8	1:05 AM: LIFEBOAT 1

Pig tune
Edith Rosenbaum played her toy musical pig to comfort children nearby.

Hide me
Daniel Buckley hid under a woman's shawl after other men were removed.

Near miss
This boat descended fast and nearly landed on Lifeboat 13.

Women only
Officer Lightoller ordered a group of men off this boat.

Window access
Passengers climbed into this boat through the windows of the promenade.

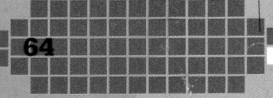

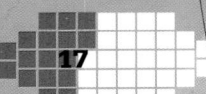

70	64	70	17	42
1:35 AM: LIFEBOAT 11	1:40 AM: LIFEBOAT 13	1:40 AM: LIFEBOAT 15	1:45 AM: LIFEBOAT 2	1:45 AM: LIFEBOAT 4

Last songs
The band played ragtime tunes and hymns on the deck outside the gym.

Lifeboats
The forward funnel broke off at 2:17, crushing some people but washing others to safety.

Launch site
Distress rockets were fired from the bridge about every five minutes.

Wave save
The collapsible canvas-sided boats A and B were stuck until a wave washed them into the water.

Rising water
By 2 AM, the water level had risen to just 3 m (10 ft) below A Deck.

A PISTOL LIKE THE ONE LOWE FIRED

Warning shots
Officer Harold Lowe saw a group of men by Lifeboat 14. "They were glaring more or less like wild beasts, ready to spring," he said. He fired his gun to warn them off. Other officers may have done the same.

Eyewitness
NAME: Nellie Becker

LIVED: 1876–1966

FROM: South Bend, Indiana, USA

DETAILS: Becker's son Richard, age one, and daughter Marion, age four, were put on Lifeboat 11, but not her daughter Ruth, age twelve. Becker cried out:

❝ Please let me in this boat! Those are my children! . . . Ruth! Get in another boat! ❞

Third-class passengers
The passengers near the bow fled their cabins as water flowed in. They grabbed their belongings and headed aft or up to higher decks.

Major help
Major Arthur Peuchen slid down a rope to help sail this boat.

26

1:10 AM: LIFEBOAT 6

Left behind
Benjamin Guggenheim is said to have watched this boat leave, then dressed in his best clothes to die.

56

1:20 AM: LIFEBOAT 9

Officer in charge
Harold Lowe took charge of this boat himself.

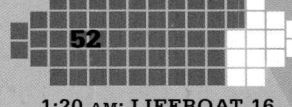

60

1:20 AM: LIFEBOAT 14

Class divide
Unusually, all passengers on this boat were second or third class.

52

1:20 AM: LIFEBOAT 16

Jumper
A man jumped into this boat as it was lowered past B Deck.

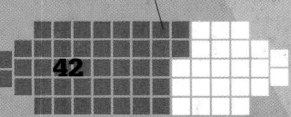

42

1:25 AM: LIFEBOAT 12

Lucky catch
A French woman fell as she boarded this boat and was caught by her ankle.

57

1:50 AM: LIFEBOAT 10

Star traveller
White Star boss Bruce Ismay got on this boat.

43

2:00 AM: COLLAPSIBLE C

Human wall
The crew linked arms to keep men off this boat.

44

2:05 AM: COLLAPSIBLE D

Wave power
The crew struggled to launch this boat; then a wave swept it out.

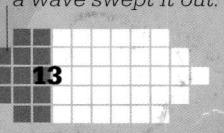

13

2:15 AM: COLLAPSIBLE A

Overturned
A wave swept this collapsible off the ship upside down.

14

2:15 AM: COLLAPSIBLE B

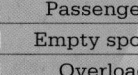

Key

■ Passenger

□ Empty spot

□ Overload

The last lifeboat

Lifeboat D was the last lifeboat to be launched from *Titanic*, at 2:05 AM. As the boat was lowered, two men jumped the 3-m (9-ft) gap from A Deck, just making it into the boat.

The occupants watched *Titanic* sink minutes later and said the Lord's Prayer as they floated in the freezing darkness. At dawn, Officer Harold Lowe, in Lifeboat 14, saw them struggling – they did not have enough passengers who could row. Lowe towed them 6.5 km (4 miles) towards *Carpathia*.

Passengers and crew included:
• Quartermaster **Arthur Bright**, who helped fire the distress rockets and loaded passengers into lifeboats before taking charge of this one.
• **Michel** and **Edmond Navratil**, two young French boys who lost their father in the disaster (see page 104).
• Five-year-old **Michael Joseph**, the other child on board, who was reunited with his mother on *Carpathia*.
• **Joseph Duquemin**, a third-class passenger who persuaded the crew to take him in from the water because he could row. He developed terrible frostbite, and his legs were later amputated.
• **Caroline Brown**, who took the last spot on the boat when her friend Edith Evans told her, "You go first. You have children waiting at home." Evans did not survive.
• **Frederick Hoyt**, who put his wife, **Jane Hoyt**, on board before the lifeboat was lowered, then jumped into the sea and climbed in, too.

Safety in sight
The flimsy canvas sides of Lifeboat D are clearly visible in this picture, taken at 7:15 AM as the lifeboat neared the rescue ship *Carpathia* after five hours at sea. Arthur Bright is at the back, using an oar as a rudder.

All alone [No help]

Radio distress messages alerted ships on the Atlantic to *Titanic*'s plight. Captain Smith hoped for help, but he knew it was too late – the ship was sinking fast.

Ice field
Any rescue mission would need time to sail around the ice field.

LENGTH OF ICE FIELD: 78 MILES (125 KM)

Ships in the area
Titanic was in a busy shipping lane, and there were other boats in the area. When *Titanic* called for assistance, *Californian* was the only ship that did not try to help (see pages 98–99).

27 km (17 miles) away
SS *Californian*
Sailing from London to Boston, its crew spotted *Titanic*. But *Californian* stopped in the ice field overnight and her radio operator went to bed.

80 km (50 miles) away
SS *Mount Temple*
Heading from Antwerp, Belgium, to Boston, this ship was blocked by the ice field.

RMS *TITANIC*
41.46 N 50.14 W

"Women and children in boats. Cannot last much longer."
—JACK PHILLIPS, RADIO OPERATOR

N
W — E
S

80 km (50 miles) away
SS *Parisian*
Parisian, sailing from Scotland to Halifax, Canada, could not pass the ice field.

127 km (79 miles) away
SS *Birma*
This slow steamer sailing from New York to Rotterdam, the Netherlands, was blocked by ice.

93 km (58 miles) away
RMS *Carpathia*
Carpathia was a Cunard liner sailing from New York to eastern Europe. Captain Rostron dodged icebergs to sail for *Titanic* at full speed.

Get ready
Rostron turned off his ship's heating to increase power to its engines, and he prepared to receive survivors.

Too far to help
Among the ships that were too far away to help was *Titanic*'s sister ship *Olympic*. The radio station at Cape Race, Canada, sent out messages seeking ships that were closer to *Titanic*.

RMS *Olympic*
800 km (500 miles) southwest, sailing from New York to Southampton

SS *Frankfurt*
225 km (140 miles) southwest, first to reply to *Titanic*'s distress calls

Cape Race
610 km (380 miles) west, a radio station for relaying messages

Last calls

Senior radio operator Jack Phillips frantically tapped out messages as *Titanic* sank. Below are some of his calls for help, and the replies. The two positions given for the ship are incorrect.

Tapping out Morse code
Radio communication was new in 1912. It took some time to send and receive messages, because they were tapped out in a code made up of dots and dashes.

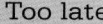

12:15 ● CQD *Titanic* 41.44 N 50.24 W.

12:17 ● CQD CQD SOS *Titanic* position 41.44 N 50.24 W. Require immediate assistance. Come at once. We struck an iceberg. Sinking.

12:20 ● Come at once. We have struck a berg. It's CQD OM. Position 41.46 N 50.14 W.

12:25 ● *Carpathia*: Shall I tell my captain? Do you require assistance?

12:26 ● Yes. Come quick.

12:32 ● *Carpathia*: Putting about and heading for you.

1:10 ● We are in collision with berg. Sinking head down. 41.46 N 50.14 W. Come soon as possible.

1:27 ● We are putting the women off in the boats.

1:45 ● Come as quickly as possible OM. Engine room is filling up to boilers.

2:17 ● CQ— (Then the signal stops as the power fades.)

Key to abbreviations
CQD = Emergency (an older distress signal)
SOS = Emergency (a new signal, adopted in 1906)
OM = Old man (a standard phrase at the time)

Too late
At 12:25 AM, Captain Smith (standing) knew that it would take four hours for help to arrive – but *Titanic* would have sunk by then.

Watch your back

The two radiomen worked until there was no more power. Assistant Harold Bride went to get Phillips's coat. He returned to find a stoker trying to steal Phillips's life jacket off his back. They punched the thief, ran to the deck, and leaped off the sinking ship.

Jack Phillips
He worked the radio non-stop until the power failed.

Harold Bride
He jumped from *Titanic* into the water with Phillips.

"Men, you have done your full duty. You can do no more. Abandon your cabin. Now it's every man for himself."
—CAPTAIN SMITH TO THE RADIOMEN, 2:05 AM

More here
For key to symbols, see page 112.

Samuel Morse Morse code radio waves **radio station North Atlantic ice field** SS *Californian*

"Nearer, My God, to Thee", **"Our God, Our Help in Ages Past"**, and **"There Is a Green Hill Far Away"** were among the popular hymns probably played by *Titanic*'s band as the ship sank.

Learn about *Titanic*'s radio room and its operators at www.hf.ro.

Read the ice warnings from other ships at www.titanic-titanic.com/warnings.shtml.

ice field: a large expanse of ice on the surface of the ocean, consisting of many ice floes and covering an area that is greater than 10 km (6 miles) across.

Morse code: a code used for transmitting messages, in which letters and numbers are represented by short or long signals.

radio: an electronic device designed to transmit and receive radio signals.

Final moments [Break-up]

It took three years to build *Titanic*, and four minutes for it to sink. At 2:17 AM, the bow sank below the surface, and the ship plunged to the seabed with 1,500 people still on board.

2:17 — Time of event

1 Bow down
Water flowed in quickly. As the bow sank beneath the surface, hundreds of people were washed into the sea.

Swept away
The last two collapsibles were swept into the sea.

Lights-out
As the bow sank, people were still trapped on the rear decks of the ship. The band played on to calm those still on board. Then all the lights flickered and went out, and *Titanic* was in darkness.

Funnel collapse
As the front funnel fell, it created a giant wave that swept people away from it.

Rise and fall
At first, the stern rose up. It fell back down when the ship tore apart.

2:18

2 The split
Titanic was built to cope with stormy, rolling seas, but the force of the iceberg crash put the thick steel beams of the keel under tremendous pressure. The force was too great, and the hull split with an explosive noise.

Breaking point
The ship broke where the keel beams split.

Pulled down
People were sucked into the funnels as they sank.

Breaking in two
The ship split at its weakest point, at the rear staircase and the engine room. These did not have strong supports.

"[The noise] was like standing under a steel railway bridge while an express train passes overhead."
—JACK THAYER, FIRST-CLASS PASSENGER

2:19

3 Break-up
Heavy with water, the flooded bow plummeted, but the stern still had enough air to float. It was forced up and out of the water.

Brief hope
As the stern settled, there was a moment when people thought it might float, but then it began to tilt again.

Deck collapse
As the ship's frame broke, the decks collapsed and crushed those still on board.

Tumbling down
As the stern rose, it tipped out furniture, pianos, and anything that was loose, including thousands of tonnes of coal, in an underwater avalanche.

Deck damage
The huge funnels carried a trail of cables that dragged down other parts of the boat.

Loose debris
Anything not bolted to the deck fell out of the smashed stern.

Eyewitness

NAME: Charles Lightoller

LIVED: 1874–1952

FROM: Southampton, UK

DETAILS: Lightoller was second officer on *Titanic*. After he organized the loading of the lifeboats, he was pulled into the water from the ship.

❝ Striking the water was like a thousand knives being driven into one's body, and, for a few moments, I completely lost grip of myself. . . . Suddenly a terrific blast of hot air came up the shaft, and blew me right away from the air shaft and up to the surface. ❞

Corkscrew course
The rudder swung to one side, making the stern spiral as it sank.

Stepping out
Chief baker Charles Joughin held onto a rail and stepped into the water as the boat sank.

Vertical stern
The stern floated upright for about a minute. Then it slid gently into the waves.

Air pockets
As air trapped in the stern was forced out, the hull was torn apart.

4 Final plunge

The stern was pushed upright and spun around before it followed the bow, plunging 3,701 m (12,144 ft) straight down to the seabed.

Falling apart
Within minutes, the two sections of *Titanic* crashed into the seabed. They landed about 610 m (2,000 ft) apart, because the bow fell at an angle of about 12 degrees, while the stern dropped vertically, like a lead weight.

Hatch crash
The forward hatch cover blew off and landed 60 m (200 ft) from the bow.

Speeding bow
The bow smashed into the seabed at about 37 kph (23 mph), sinking 18 m (60 ft) into the silt.

Shattered plates
The large steel plates that covered the hull broke off as the ship was torn apart.

Debris field
Thousands of objects falling from Titanic were scattered across an area of about 5.2 sq km (2 sq. miles).

Titanic came to rest on the seabed 3.7 km (2.3 miles) down

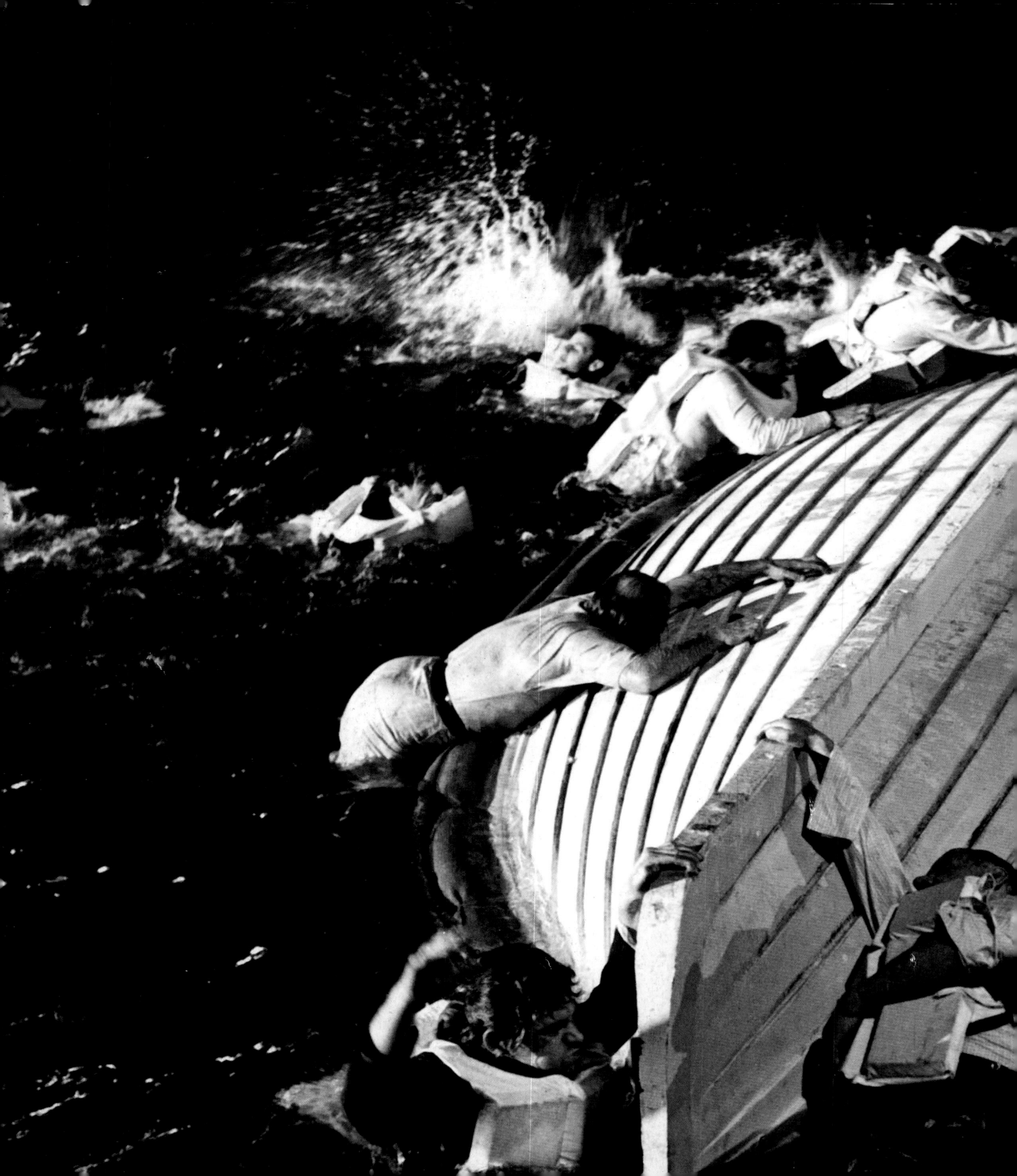

Last chance

As *Titanic* sank, collapsible Lifeboat B was washed upside-down into the freezing sea. Radioman Harold Bride found himself in an air pocket beneath it, and he managed to climb onto the overturned hull. He joined 30 other people who were standing on the boat or clinging to its sides. The boat sank lower in the water as the air pocket leaked away, and waves washed over the survivors as the boat rocked. Some of them died, and their bodies slipped into the dark water. Officer Charles Lightoller instructed the desperate group to lean against the direction of the rolling to keep the boat afloat through the night.

Meanwhile, Fifth Officer Harold Lowe moved people from Lifeboat 14 into another boat and gathered a crew of eight men to look for survivors. He was afraid that their boat would be turned over if too many people tried to climb in, so he waited. At about 3:20 AM, he returned. His lamp shone on a mass of dead bodies held up by their life jackets. Lowe hauled four more people aboard, but one died almost immediately. Lifeboat 14 was the only one of *Titanic*'s lifeboats that went back in search of survivors (see page 99).

Desperate struggle
The scene of survivors climbing onto the overturned Lifeboat B was recreated for the 1958 film *A Night to Remember*.

Lost
fou

* Why couldn't Harold Bride walk off *Carpathia*?

* What did US senators say about the sinking?

* Who received money to return to England?

and nd

Rescued [Terrible wait]

Carpathia found *Titanic*'s lifeboats floating among huge icebergs in the early morning of 15 April. The cold survivors were taken on board, and the liner sailed to New York. Soon the tragic story of the sinking and the massive loss of life became a worldwide sensation.

Long wait

Lifeboat 2 was the first to reach *Carpathia*, at 4:10 AM. It took hours to find the other boats and bring 707 people on board. Sadly, three people had died on the lifeboats, and another died on *Carpathia*.

Rescue ship
Carpathia's public rooms became dormitories, and the three dining rooms were used as first-aid stations, one for each class.

All lost
Carpathia's passengers donated clothing and helped treat the shocked, freezing survivors after their terrifying night in open boats.

Confusion

During the four days of *Carpathia*'s journey to New York, survivors' names were radioed to land and released to the public. But this took time. Meanwhile, newspapers ran stories that were often sensational and inaccurate.

Messages home
It took days for operators on *Carpathia* to radio the names of survivors.

Newspaper frenzy
Journalists, eager for exclusive news, offered big money to tell survivors' stories.

Who survived?
New York crowds were desperate for news. No one knew how *Titanic* could have sunk.

Eyewitness

NAME: Charlotte Collyer

LIVED: 1880–1914

FROM: Basingstoke, UK

DETAILS: Like many wives taken to *Carpathia*, Collyer hoped her husband had survived the disaster.

" We could only rush frantically from group to group, searching the haggard faces, crying out names. . . . I had a husband to search for. . . . I had believed [he] would be found in one of the boats. He was not there. "

CHARLOTTE COLLYER

Late arrival

Carpathia arrived in New York at 9:30 PM on 18 April. Each passenger class left separately, and it was 11 PM before third-class survivors touched dry land.

Crippled by the cold
Radio operator Harold Bride (centre) had to be carried from the ship because he could not walk on his frozen, bandaged feet. The *New York Times* paid £100 (£9,000 today) for his story.

Families fear t

A crowd studies the list
survivors, posted outsid
Southampton office. Far
days for news, and a loc
said that he "heard mar
of loved ones aboard th
vessel, who in many cas
breadwinners of the fam
720 of *Titanic*'s 899 crew
were from Southampto
three were men. Only 1

Saved and lost [Too many]

Of the 2,223 people on *Titanic*, only 706 reached New York – most of them women and children. Many families were left without husbands and fathers to support them. The crew's pay was stopped. Here, find out what happened to some of the people you met earlier in this book.

706 saved; 1,517 lost
(crew and passengers)

Saved

"Women and children first" meant that 75 percent of the women and 50 percent of the children lived. The crew members who were in charge of sailing the lifeboats also survived.

MARGARET BROWN
(See page 49.)

HAROLD LOWE
(See pages 60, 79, and 81.)

STUART COLLETT
(See page 54.)

Poor crew

Their pay stopped the second *Titanic* sank, so many of the crew had to appeal to the public for funds.

TITANIC **CREW AT COURT BEFORE THE UK INQUIRY**

Charlotte Collyer

Collyer and her daughter received relief funds and £60 – equivalent to £5,400 today – for a magazine article, which helped them return to England. (See pages 71 and 91.)

EVA & ESTHER HART
(See pages 55 and 76.)

FREDERICK FLEET
(See pages 69 and 71.)

Douglas Spedden

Young Spedden and the rest of his family were saved. (See pages 66–67.)

Archibald Gracie

Gracie was dragged down "in a whirlpool of water, swirling round and round." A strong swimmer, he fought his way to the surface and found a spot in a lifeboat. (See page 98.)

JOSEPH BOXHALL
(See page 60.)

Class divide

It is hard to determine who lived and who died, because papers were lost at sea. These numbers are the ones confirmed at the US inquiry (see pages 96–97). Passengers on the upper decks had a better chance of reaching the lifeboats. Crew members sailing the boats rescued some of their shipmates from the sea.

Numbers
Survivors are shown in the top bars; those who died are below.

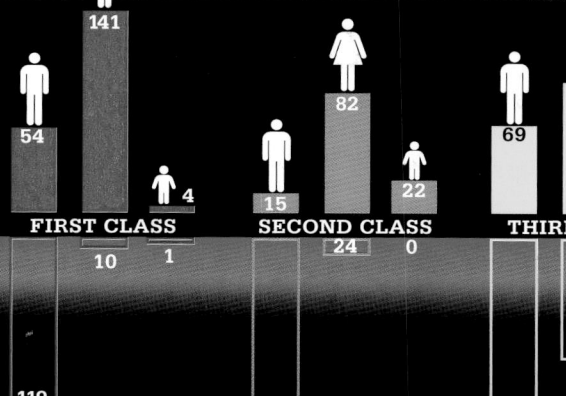

FIRST CLASS		SECOND CLASS		THIRD CLASS		CREW
54	141	82	15	69	74	141
	4		22		31	
10	1	24	0			52
119		142		67		
				417		685

Lost

Some people put loved ones on lifeboats, then stayed on *Titanic*. Others, such as Jack Phillips, found a boat but died at sea. Every death was a tragedy.

JACK PHILLIPS *(See pages 70–71, 77, and 83.)*

Isidor and Ida Straus
Ida Straus refused to leave her husband to take a place in a lifeboat, so both died. (See pages 52 and 78.)

Death duties
All the musicians died, and their families were billed for lost uniforms.

Benjamin Guggenheim
This millionaire put on his fine clothes and said that he and his valet were "prepared to go down like gentlemen". (See pages 53 and 79.)

Thomas Andrews
Titanic's designer did not try to save himself and was last seen staring at a picture in the first-class smoking room. (See pages 34 and 77.)

Lost crew
Engineers died trying to save the ship by keeping the water from pouring in.

THE GOODWIN FAMILY *(See pages 56–57.)*

SIDNEY GOODWIN AND HIS SHOES

Sidney Goodwin
Sidney was the 19-month-old baby left out of the family picture at above right. The whole family died, and Sidney's shoes are now in a museum.

JOHN STARR MARCH *(See page 58.)*

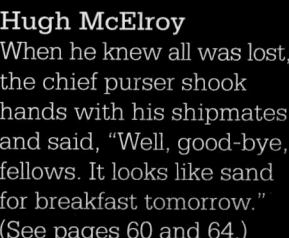

WILLIAM MURDOCH *(See page 60.)*

Hugh McElroy
When he knew all was lost, the chief purser shook hands with his shipmates and said, "Well, good-bye, fellows. It looks like sand for breakfast tomorrow." (See pages 60 and 64.)

British inquiry
The inquiry, from 2 May to 3 July 1912, concluded that the sinking was "brought about by the excessive speed at which the ship was being navigated."

Heroes and villains

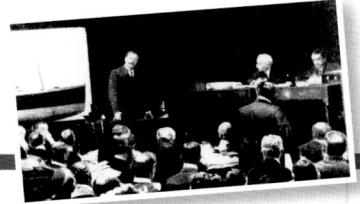

Two inquiries and hundreds of newspaper stories cast some of *Titanic*'s passengers and crew as heroes or villains. Many of the survivors sold their stories to the press, and some gave evidence at the inquiries.

Heroes

Amazing stories of people's calm bravery in the panic and confusion of *Titanic*'s final hours emerged. Officer Charles Lightoller helped passengers onto lifeboats, then fell into the sea near an overturned collapsible. He was the last survivor to board *Carpathia*. Other heroes were passengers who helped steer boats or stepped off lifeboats to make room for others.

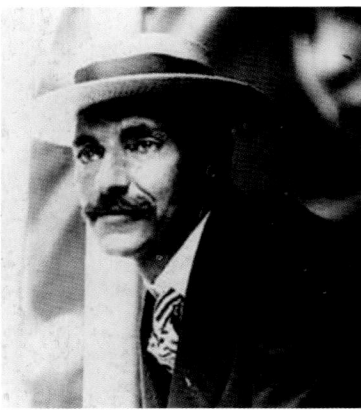

John Jacob Astor
Barred from his wife's lifeboat, Astor called out to comfort her as her boat was lowered.

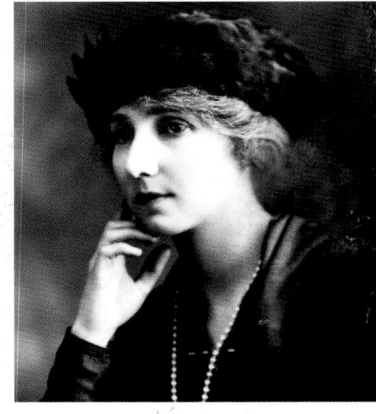

Countess of Rothes
Noël Leslie steered Lifeboat 8 all night long, unlike others who let the crew do the work.

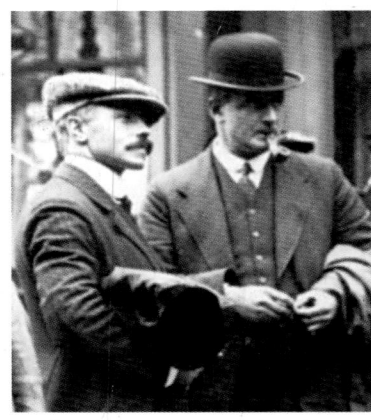

Officer Charles Lightoller
Lightoller (right) helped people off the ship, then kept a lifeboat afloat in the sea, saving more.

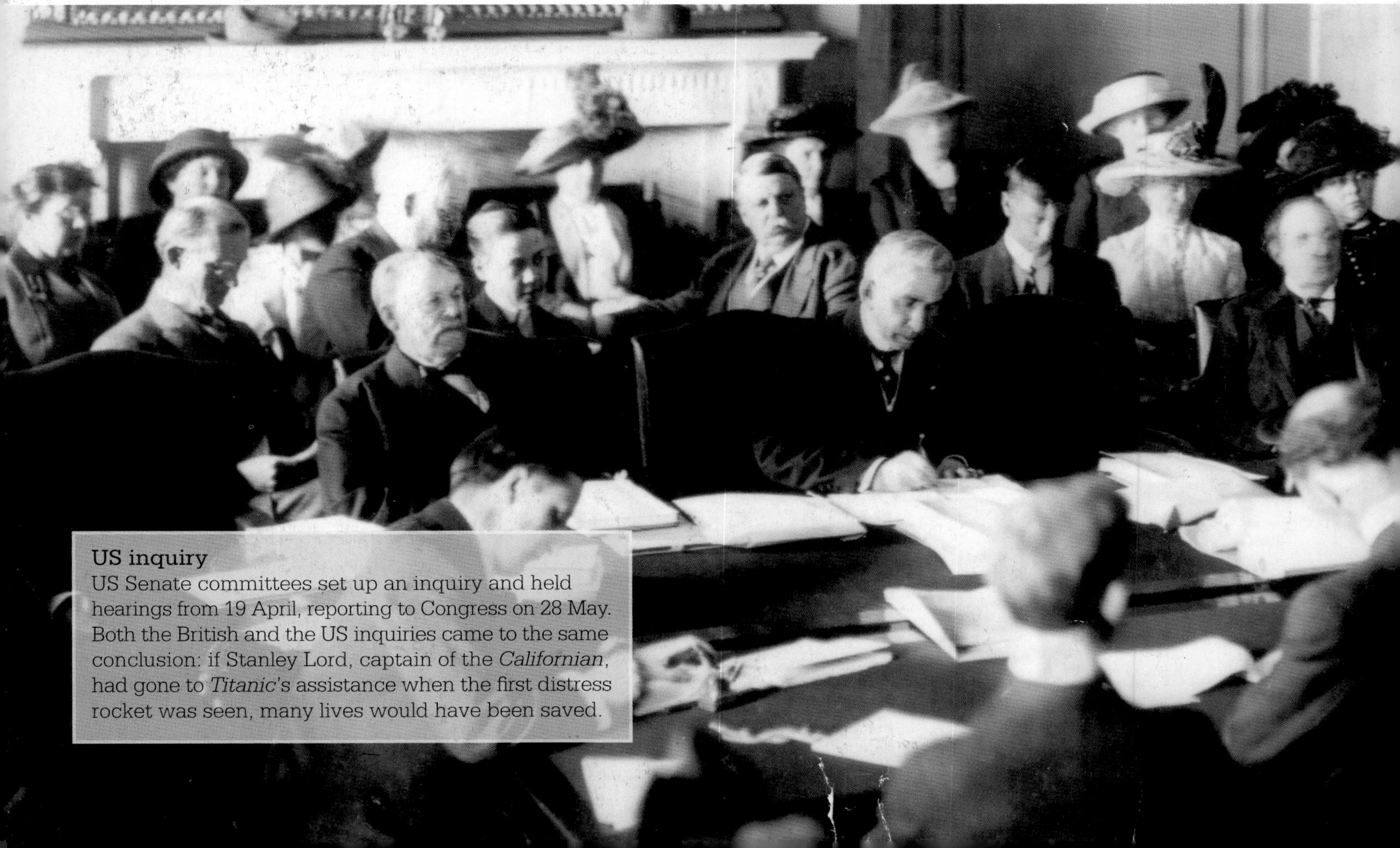

US inquiry
US Senate committees set up an inquiry and held hearings from 19 April, reporting to Congress on 28 May. Both the British and the US inquiries came to the same conclusion: if Stanley Lord, captain of the *Californian*, had gone to *Titanic*'s assistance when the first distress rocket was seen, many lives would have been saved.

Villains

The media named three main villains: Stanley Lord, captain of the *Californian* (see page 99); Cosmo Duff Gordon, a passenger who was accused of bribing crew; and Bruce Ismay, one of *Titanic*'s owners, who got into a lifeboat and left others to die. He said, "I took the chance when it came to me."

Bruce Ismay
Ismay was condemned as a coward by the press and the public after he saved himself.

Cosmo Duff Gordon
Duff Gordon gave the crew on his lifeboat £5 each, supposedly as a bribe to not row back for survivors.

Captain Smith: hero or villain?

Opinions were divided over *Titanic*'s captain. Was he to blame for speeding into an ice field, or a hero for organizing the lifeboats without saving himself?

"His indifference to danger was one of the direct and contributing causes of this unnecessary tragedy."

—SENATOR WILLIAM ALDEN SMITH, TALKING ABOUT CAPTAIN SMITH AT THE US INQUIRY ON 28 MAY 1912

"He was doing only that which other skilled men would have done in the same position."

—SIR JOHN CHARLES BIGHAM, AT THE BRITISH INQUIRY, POINTING OUT THAT CRUISING AT HIGH SPEED AT NIGHT WAS THE USUAL PRACTICE

"Had Capt. Smith been on the bridge, I am confident that the horrible accident would have been averted. . . . At seven o'clock on the night of the accident the captain went to a dinner party in full dress and stayed until nine or ten-thirty, and I am at a loss to understand why a captain with 2,000 souls in his care, and in a ship approaching icebergs, should dine in a restaurant in that way."

—MAJOR ARTHUR PEUCHEN, FIRST-CLASS PASSENGER, IN A NEWSPAPER INTERVIEW

Smith memorial
This statue honouring Smith is inscribed with his alleged last words: "Be British."

Big questions

Over the years, many books and articles have been written about the night that *Titanic* sank. Theories have been proposed and arguments have raged about exactly how and why the disaster occurred. At least four big questions remain.

Big story
This eastern European stamp, depicting an artist's impression of *Titanic*'s sinking, shows that the story of the disaster was known around the world.

The ice warnings question

Ice ahead
It was unusual to find ice as far south as *Titanic*'s route.

Should Captain Smith have paid more attention to the ice warnings from other ships? Keep in mind that the route was further south than where icebergs normally floated, and the warnings that officers received did not mention ice directly ahead. Also, one message never reached the bridge at all, because the radio operators were so busy.

"There had been an extremely mild winter in the Arctic, owing to which, ice from the ice cap and glaciers had broken away in phenomenal quantities. . . . In my fifteen years' experience . . . I had certainly never seen anything like it."

—OFFICER CHARLES LIGHTOLLER, IN HIS 1935 AUTOBIOGRAPHY, TITANIC *AND OTHER SHIPS*

"With the atmosphere literally charged with warning signals and wireless messages registering their last appeal, the stokers in the engine room fed their fires with fresh fuel, registering in that dangerous place her fastest speed."

—SENATOR WILLIAM ALDEN SMITH, AT THE US INQUIRY ON 28 MAY 1912

The speed question

Should *Titanic* have been moving more slowly?
It sped through the night at 22.5 knots (42 kph / 26 mph). But this was a normal speed for transatlantic liners, which had tight deadlines to meet. However, on that night, the other transatlantic ships had slowed down or even stopped because of the ice warnings.

"Towards evening the report, which I heard, was spread that wireless messages from passing steamers had been received advising the officers of our ship of the presence of icebergs. . . . No diminution of speed was indicated and the engines kept up their steady running."

—COLONEL ARCHIBALD GRACIE, FIRST-CLASS PASSENGER, IN HIS 1913 BOOK, *THE TRUTH ABOUT THE* TITANIC

"Every captain who has run full speed through fog and iceberg regions is to blame for the disaster as much as [Captain Smith] is: they got through and he did not."

—LAWRENCE BEESLEY, SECOND-CLASS PASSENGER

The *Californian* question

Could *Californian* have helped? *Californian* was the ship nearest to *Titanic* at the time of the sinking. It had lifeboat spaces for 218 people and could have shuttled many more passengers to safety. But the radioman had gone to bed. *Californian*'s crew spotted *Titanic*'s distress rockets, but the captain, Stanley Lord, said that he thought they were a greeting between ships from the same company.

"When we passed one of our own steamers, we would salute them by firing a distress rocket. . . . It was the height of every shipmaster's ambition in those days, and officers and crew too, to pick up a ship in distress. . . . If we'd had any sign of anything like that, we'd have been after it like a shot."

—CAPTAIN STANLEY LORD

CAPTAIN LORD

The ship on the horizon
Passengers and crew on *Titanic* saw the lights of a ship on the horizon. Captain Smith told the lifeboats to row towards it, but the ship disappeared from sight. It was *Californian*.

Sea regulations at the time stated that if a ship saw "rockets or shells, throwing stars of any colour or description, fired one at a time, at short intervals," it must offer help to the ship in distress.

The US inquiry concluded that *Californian*'s "officers and crew saw the distress signals of the *Titanic* and failed to respond to them."

The lifeboats question

Why didn't the lifeboats collect more passengers from the water? There weren't enough lifeboat seats for everyone on board *Titanic*, and in the confusion many boats were launched only half full. Then the lifeboats were rowed away quickly, to avoid being sucked down with *Titanic*. Hundreds of people still on *Titanic* were thrown into the freezing water as the ship sank, but only one lifeboat returned to help.

"As soon as the ship disappeared I said: 'Now, men, we will pull towards the wreck.' Everyone in my boat said it was a mad idea because we had far better save what few I had in my boat than go back to the scene of the wreck and be swamped."

—HERBERT PITMAN, THIRD OFFICER

"There they were, only four or five hundred yards away, listening to the cries, and still they did not come back. If they had turned back several hundred more would have been saved."

—JACK THAYER, FIRST-CLASS PASSENGER

Last of the boats
Carpathia carried some of *Titanic*'s lifeboats to New York harbour and dropped them off at the Cunard pier there.

Found [Miles down]

The broken wreck of *Titanic* lay scattered across the seabed for 73 years. No one knew exactly where it was or had the right equipment to search so deep.

Wreckage trail

Marine scientist Robert Ballard found *Titanic*. He searched for debris by towing an unmanned deep-sea vehicle, equipped with cameras, from a ship.

Alvin the submersible
Ballard visited the wreck site in *Alvin*, a deep-sea diving craft that held crew.

Detailed study
In 2004, Ballard used two underwater robots, steered from a ship floating above.

Film crew
This robot camera had powerful lights to film in the dark.

Hard to find

The last position given by *Titanic* before it sank was wrong, so explorers could only guess the correct location of the wreck. And it lies too deep underwater for divers to reach alone.

1985 French scientists, working with Ballard, dragged a scanner near the wreck site and found the debris field.

1986 Ballard visited the wreck in the *Alvin* submersible.

1987 Explorers salvaged objects from the site. This continued for years.

1995 Film director James Cameron filmed the site, using some of the shots in his 1997 movie, *Titanic*.

1998 A large piece of the hull was recovered, two years after the first salvage attempt had failed.

2010 The whole site was mapped using sonar.

Explorers took more than
6,000
objects from the site

Effects of time

Titanic is falling apart. Sea creatures have eaten most of the wood. Metal is being destroyed by salt, water pressure, and rust. And bacteria and fungi hang from surfaces like icicles.

Robbing a grave?

Dives into the *Titanic* wreck have brought thousands of artifacts to the surface. These include plates and cups, as well as items that belonged to the dead. Some people consider this robbing a grave.

Surviving items
Clothes, glasses, bags, and watches are all that remain of those who died on *Titanic*.

POCKET WATCH

GLADSTONE BAG

More here

For key to symbols, see page 112.

***Finding the* Titanic**
by Robert D. Ballard

***Secrets of the* Titanic**
is a 1986 documentary
about finding the wreck.

***Deep Inside the* Titanic**
is a 1999 film that explores
the wreck site.

**"It Was Sad When that
Great Ship Went Down"**
is a folk song about the
sinking. Other songs include
"The Wreck of the *Titanic*"
by Jeff Calhoun, from 1927,
and **"Down with the Old
Canoe"** by the Dixon
Brothers, from 1938.

Visit **Titanic** in Branson,
Missouri, USA, which is a
replica of the ship, and
Titanic in Pigeon Forge,
Tennessee, USA, which
also exhibits artifacts in
a ship-shaped museum.

salvage: to recover
something from a wreck.

sonar: a method of finding
underwater objects by
reflecting sound waves
off them.

submersible: a vessel that
can travel underwater.

Sea view
These are the windows of
a first-class cabin on the
port side of the boat deck.

SPECTACLES

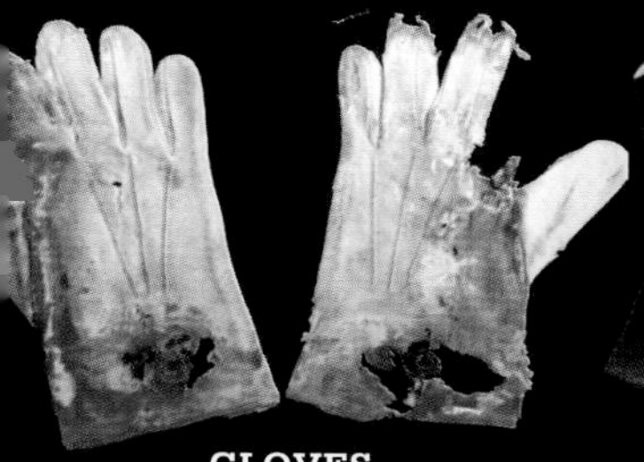

GLOVES

VEST

All that remains
This pair of boots marks
where a body landed.
Only the leather
footwear survives.

At rest

This is *Titanic's* bow. It fell 3.7 km
(2.3 miles) to the seabed, where its
sharp edge plunged into the silt like a
knife. Microbes have eaten away at the
steel plating on the hull and created
strangely shaped rust formations.
This photograph was taken in 2004
by scientists on a research expedition.

Survivors [Amazing stories]

The survivors of *Titanic* were affected by the disaster forever. Some became celebrities, others lost everything, and many had to start new lives alone.

Orphans of the deep

Michel Navratil had separated from his French wife and kidnapped their sons. He gave them false names on *Titanic* – Loto and Louis Hoffman (see page 54) – so when he died, no one knew who the boys were. Newspapers called them the "orphans of the deep".

Navratil brothers
Michel was three and Edmond was two when they were rescued (see page 81). Survivor Margaret Hays looked after the boys in New York.

Reunited
Newspaper reports eventually reached their mother, Marcelle, and she was reunited with her sons in New York on 16 May.

Lost a fortune
Madeleine Astor (see pages 49 and 59) inherited a fortune when her husband died on *Titanic*. She survived, and gave birth to their son. But four years later she gave up the money to marry again.

Sportsman in love
Tennis star and first-class passenger Karl Behr married Helen Newsom a year after the sinking. He had followed Newsom onto *Titanic* to persuade her to marry him.

Last survivor
Millvina Dean was a baby on *Titanic*, travelling third class. Her mother and brother survived, but her father died. Later she became known for appearances at *Titanic* events. She was the last survivor to die, in 2009.

Left behind
Two years after the sinking, Lucile Carter divorced her husband. He had boarded a lifeboat and left her for dead on *Titanic*.

Road casualty
The Spedden family (see pages 66–67) made it to New York, but young Douglas died in 1915 after being struck by a car.

Starring role
Leading actress Dorothy Gibson played herself in a film about the sinking, made just four weeks later. In the movie, Gibson wore the same white silk dress she had worn on the night of the disaster.

The ship that survived
Another survivor was *Titanic*'s sister ship *Olympic*. Fitted with extra lifeboats and proper watertight compartments, it served as a liner until 1935. During World War I, it was used as a troopship and earned the nickname "Old Reliable".

aft
Close to or towards the stern, or rear, of a ship.

apprentice
A person learning to do skilled labour. Some apprentices were legally bound to an employer or craftsman for a period of time in order to learn a trade.

aristocrat
A person who is a member of the highest social class in a particular society.

ballast
Heavy material, such as gravel, sand, or iron, that is placed in the bottom of a ship to stabilize it. The ballast may be redistributed or removed to change its effect on the movement of the ship.

bankrupt
Lacking money and unable to pay off any debts.

berth
A place to sit or sleep on a ship. A two-berth cabin has two beds in it.

boilermaker
A person who makes or repairs boilers or other heavy metal items.

bow
The front end of a ship.

breadwinner
A person who supports a family with his or her earnings.

bribe
To persuade someone to do something by offering or promising money or a gift.

bridge
The platform from which a ship is piloted and navigated.

bunker
A large container or compartment for storing fuel such as coal.

cargo
Goods or merchandise carried on a ship.

chart
A map used by navigators on a ship to determine its course.

chauffeur
A person employed by a wealthy person or family to drive a car.

chronometer
A very accurate clock that is not affected by the movement of a ship or by changes in air pressure, temperature, or the atmosphere.

compass
An instrument for finding direction, usually with a magnetized needle that turns on a pivot and points to the magnetic north.

crow's nest
A partly enclosed platform at or near the top of a ship's mast, used by a lookout to spot approaching danger.

current
A steady flow in a particular direction in a body of water.

davit
A crane-like machine used to raise and lower objects such as lifeboats over the side of a ship or a hatchway.

debris
The remains of something that has broken up.

disembark
To go ashore from a ship.

draughtsman
A person who draws plans of machinery that will be built.

dry dock
A place where a ship is repaired or painted. After the ship has sailed into the dry dock, the water in the dock is pumped out. The dock is filled with water again when the ship is ready to leave.

emigrant
A person who leaves his or her country to live in another country.

engineer
A person trained in the design, construction, and use of engines or machines.

evacuate
To remove from a dangerous place to somewhere safer.

famine
A serious lack of food in a region because of a disaster such as war or a drought.

firn
Grainy snow on the upper part of a glacier, where it has not yet been compressed into ice.

forge
To heat and hammer metal in order to change its shape.

found
To establish a new company.

founder
To fill with water and sink.

TITANIC IN DRY DOCK

Glossary

frostbite
The freezing of parts of the body, usually the ears, nose, fingers, and toes.

funnel
A metal chimney on a steamship through which smoke and exhaust gases from the boilers escape.

gantry
A bridge-like overhead structure with a platform that supports equipment such as cranes. A gantry acts as a supporting framework while a ship is being built.

glacier
A slow-moving river of compacted ice, formed by layers of snow that build up on mountains or near the North and South Poles.

greaser
A person who greases, or lubricates, a ship's engines.

hull
The main body of a ship, not including the masts, sails, rigging, engines, or other fittings.

ice field
A large expanse of ice on the surface of the ocean, consisting of many ice floes and covering an area that is greater than 10 km (6 miles) across.

immigrant
A person who comes to live and work permanently in a foreign country.

inquiry
An official investigation into an accident or event, often held in a public place.

isolate
To keep a sick person separate from other people.

keel
A long piece of wood or metal that runs along the bottom of the hull of a ship like a backbone. The ship's frames are attached to it.

latitude
Distance north or south of the Equator, measured in degrees. Imaginary lines of latitude are drawn horizontally around the globe.

life jacket
A buoyant vest that keeps a person afloat in water.

liner
A large, luxurious ship operated by a shipping company along a regular route.

logo
A symbol or picture that identifies a company or product.

longitude
Distance east or west of the prime meridian—an imaginary line that runs vertically through Greenwich, London—measured in degrees. Lines of longitude are drawn on the globe from the North Pole to the South Pole.

maiden voyage
The first journey of a new ship.

marconigram
A message sent via a Marconi radio.

migration
The movement of people across land or oceans to find new places to live or work.

Morse code
A code used for transmitting messages, in which letters and numbers are represented by short or long signals. The code was invented in 1838 by Samuel Morse.

navigator
An officer on a ship who finds the way from one place to another by using the Sun, the stars, and special instruments.

persecution
A campaign of hostility and ill-treatment conducted because of the politics, race, or religious beliefs of a person or group.

port
The left-hand side of a ship when looking forwards, towards the bow.

porthole
A window, usually round, in a ship's hull.

poverty
The state of being very poor and unable to buy food or other essential items.

WATCH RECOVERED FROM *TITANIC*'S WRECK

prejudice
A hostile opinion about or attitude towards people of other races or religions. Prejudices are usually formed unjustly, without accurate information or proper reasoning.

promenade
A public place for strolling for pleasure or display. Promenades were very popular in Europe at the beginning of the 20th century.

propeller
A central shaft with attached blades that rotate as the shaft turns. This movement drives a ship forwards in water.

purser
An officer on a ship who deals with financial matters and keeps accounts. He looks after money and valuables for passengers and is responsible for their comfort and welfare. The chief purser on *Titanic* was in charge of the stewards.

"It was truly a lovely ship and at that time we felt very lucky to have been able to book passage on her."

—ROBERTHA JOSEPHINE WATT, SECOND-CLASS PASSENGER, AGE 12 WHEN SHE TRAVELLED

quartermaster
An officer who steers a ship and has other navigational duties, including signaling.

quoits
A game in which circles of rope are thrown at a target.

radio
An electronic device designed to transmit and receive radio signals through the air via radio waves. It converts electric impulses into sound.

rivet
A metal bolt that holds two or more metal plates together. The bolt is passed through a hole in each plate and then beaten or pressed down when in place.

rudder
A flat, hinged piece of wood or metal used to steer a ship. This underwater blade is positioned at the stern of a ship. When it is turned, it causes the ship's bow to turn in the same direction.

salvage
To recover something from a wreck.

sextant
A navigational instrument used to determine the latitude and longitude of a ship at sea and to set its course. It measures the angle between the horizon and the Sun, the Moon, or a particular star or pattern of stars.

shift
A working period of several hours. Shifts enable different groups of workers to do the same job at different times of the day.

shuffleboard
A game in which standing players use long cues to push wooden disks into numbered areas marked on a smooth surface, such as the deck of a ship.

slipway
A sloping surface that runs down into water. Slipways are used to launch or land ships when building or repairing them.

sonar
A method of finding underwater objects. It involves sending out pulses of sound, then detecting and measuring their return after they have been reflected off other objects. *Sonar* stands for *SOund NAvigation and Ranging.*

starboard
The right-hand side of a ship when looking forwards, towards the bow.

stern
The back end of a ship. The stern is at the opposite end of the ship from the bow.

steward
A man whose job is to look after passengers on a ship. A woman who does the same job is called a stewardess.

stoker
A person who stokes, or feeds, a furnace with fuel such as coal in order to run the engines of a ship. On British ships, a stoker is sometimes called a fireman.

submersible
A vessel that can travel underwater. Submersibles are often used for research and exploration in the depth of the oceans.

taffrail log
An instrument used to calculate the speed of a ship through the water. A rotating device is attached to a reading unit and towed through the water from the railing at the ship's stern.

tenement
A run-down and often overcrowded apartment building, usually in a poor section of a large city.

transmitter
The part of a radio that converts sound waves into electric waves.

trimmer
A person who works in the engine room of a ship, shoveling coal and delivering it to the stokers.

LIFE JACKET

turbine
A wheel with blades that, when spun rapidly, drives a machine to make electricity.

Turkish bath
A bath in which the bather visits a series of steam rooms of increasing temperature, then takes a cold shower and has a massage.

valet
A male servant who looks after his wealthy employer, including taking care of his clothing.

> **Don't be so ridiculous. Even if we have grazed an iceberg it can't do any serious damage with all these watertight compartments. . . . Go back to bed and don't worry.**
>
> —SIR COSMO DUFF GORDON TO HIS WIFE, LUCY

Index

PHOTOGRAPHY AND ARTWORK

1: Harland & Wolff, Ulster Folk & Transport Museum/National Museums Northern Ireland (NMNI); 2–3: White Star Photo Library; 4–5 (background): Zacarias Pereira da Mata/Shutterstock; 6: Harland & Wolff, Ulster Folk & Transport Museum/National Museums Northern Ireland (NMNI); 7l: Hulton Archive/Getty Images; 7cl: Tim Loughhead/Precision Illustration; 7cr: Popperfoto/Getty Images; 7r: akg-images; 8–9: World History Archive/Image Asset Management Ltd/Alamy Images; 10–11: Ralph White/Corbis Images; 12l: Gorgios/Dreamstime; 12c: Detroit Publishing Co. No. 036490/Gift, State Historical Society of Colorado, 1949/Library of Congress; 12r: Hulton Archive/Getty Images; 14–15 (main image): Popperfoto/Getty Images; 14cl: ITV Global/The Picture Desk; 14cm: 20th Century Fox/Paramount/The Picture Desk; 15tc: White Star Photo Library; 15cr: Le Site du *Titanic*/Wikipedia; 16tr: Science Museum/Science and Society Picture Library; 16 (emigrants): American Stereoscopic Co./Library of Congress; 16 (gantry): George Grantham Bain Collection/Library of Congress; 16 (White Star logo): Whistlerpro/Wikipedia; 16bl: Images of American Political History/Wikipedia; 16 (*Titanic*'s launch): White Star Photo Library; 16 (crowd): solid-istanbul/iStockphoto; 17tl: Father Frank Browne/Fr Browne SJ Collection/UIG/Bridgeman Art Library; 17tr: George Grantham Bain Collection/Library of Congress; 17 (iceberg): Logray-2008/iStockphoto; 17bl: Library of Congress; 17br: NOAA/Institute for Exploration/University of Rhode Island (NOAA/IFE/URI)/Wikipedia; 18 (map): Nicemonkey/Shutterstock; 18 (paddles): from *Maritime New York in Nineteenth-Century Photographs* by Harry Johnson and Frederick S. Lightfoot, Dover Publications, New York, 1980, page 14, from a stereogram by George Stacy/Wikipedia; 18 (propeller): Hemera/Thinkstock; 18 (*Great Western*, *Great Britain*): Tony Fernandes; 18–19 (propeller icon): jangeltun/iStockphoto; 19 (*Teutonic*): De Agostini Picture Library/Getty Images; 19 (*Kaiser*): Mesanthroppee@DeviantArt; 19 (*Mauretania*, *Olympic*, *Titanic*): Simon Glancey/wwrgallery.co.uk; 20 (main image): Gorgios/Dreamstime; 20bl: Whistlerpro/Wikipedia; 20bc: Universal Images Group/Getty Images; 21 (main image): NRM/Pictorial Collection/Science and Society Picture Library; 21tr: Tim Loughhead/Precision Illustration; 21bc: Wikipedia; 21br: Cunard Line; 22–23: Hulton Archive/Getty Images; 24–25 (map): Nicemonkey/Shutterstock; 24 (statue silhouettes): ziggymaj/iStockphoto; 24cl: Lewis Wickes Hine/Library of Congress; 24bl: Detroit Publishing Co. no. 036490/Gift, State Historical Society of Colorado, 1949/Library of Congress; 24br: Bkkbrad/Wikipedia; 25tl: from the preface to the first edition of *An Illustrated History of Ireland from AD 400 to 1800* by Mary Frances Cusack, illustrated by Henry Doyle/Wikipedia; 25bl: Library of Congress; 25bc: OGphoto/iStockphoto; 25br: Stephen Chernin/AP Images; 26–27 (main image): Dennis Puleston/Science Source; 26cl: Claus Lunau/Science Photo Library/Science Source; 26bc: Bernhard Edmaier/Science Source; 26br: Digital Vision/Thinkstock; 27tr: pkline/iStockphoto; 27bl: bbuong/iStockphoto; 27bc: GeoEye/Science Photo Library/Science Source; 27br: Photos.com/Thinkstock; 28l: Tim Loughhead/Precision Illustration; 28c: Harland & Wolff, Ulster Folk & Transport Museum/National Museums Northern Ireland (NMNI); 28r: White Star Photo Library; 30tr: okänt/Wikipedia; 30cl: CrazyPhunk/Wikipedia; 30b: White Star Photo Library; 31 (main image): Tim Loughhead/Precision Illustration; 31blt: White Star Photo Library; 31blc, 31blb: Harland & Wolff, Ulster Folk & Transport Museum/National Museums Northern Ireland (NMNI); 32–33 (main image): Tim Loughhead/Precision Illustration; 33tl: Miaow Miaow/Wikipedia; 33tr: Harland & Wolff, Ulster Folk & Transport Museum/National Museums Northern Ireland (NMNI); 34–35t: from *Engineering*, "The White Star liner *Titanic*," Vol. 91/Wikipedia; 34–35 (coins): LdF/iStockphoto; 34tr, 34bl: Harland & Wolff, Ulster Folk & Transport Museum/National Museums Northern Ireland (NMNI); 34bc: Tiero/Dreamstime; 34br: Tormentor/Dreamstime; 35b, 36–37: Harland & Wolff, Ulster Folk & Transport Museum/National Museums Northern Ireland (NMNI); 38–39: White Star Photo Library; 40–41 (deck plan): Tim Loughhead/Precision Illustration; 40 (poop deck, Café Parisien), 41tl: White Star Photo Library; 41tc: Father Browne/Universal Images Group/Getty Images; 41tr: White Star Photo Library; 42–43 (deck plan): Tim Loughhead/Precision Illustration; 42 (engines, barber shop): White Star Photo Library; 43tl: English School/The Bridgeman Art Library/Getty Images; 43tc, 43tr: White Star Photo Library; 44–45 (background): Zacarias Pereira da Mata/Shutterstock; 44c: jimd_stock/iStockphoto; 44r: Sang Tan/AP Images; 45tr: Hulton-Deutsch Collection/Corbis Images; 46l: George Grantham Bain Collection/Library of Congress; 46c: dja65/iStockphoto; 46r: Tim Loughhead/Precision Illustration; 48: Father Frank Browne/Fr Browne SJ Collection/UIG/Bridgeman Art Library; 49 (background): Wikipedia; 49tr: Father Frank Browne/Fr Browne SJ Collection/UIG/Bridgeman Art Library; 49 (London silhouette): Leontura/iStockphoto; 49bl: Father Frank Browne/Fr Browne SJ Collection/UIG/Bridgeman Art Library; 49br: George Grantham Bain Collection/Library of Congress; 50 (person icons): Leremy/Shutterstock; 50tl: Father Browne/Universal Images Group/Getty Images; 50cl: Joe Knapp; 50bl: White Star Photo Library; 50 (Lady Duff Gordon): George Grantham Bain Collection/Library of Congress; 50 (Sir Duff Gordon): Topical Press Agency/Stringer/Getty Images; 51, 52–53: White Star Photo Library; 53tr: Tim Loughhead/Precision Illustration; 53cr: Harland & Wolff, Ulster Folk & Transport Museum/National Museums Northern Ireland (NMNI); 53br: Wikipedia; 54tl: Bain News Service/Flickr Commons Project 2008/Library of Congress; 54tc: mateu/iStockphoto; 54cl, 54bl: White Star Photo Library; 54 (person icons): Leremy/Shutterstock; 54r: George Grantham Bain Collection/Library of Congress; 55: Harland & Wolff, Ulster Folk & Transport Museum/National Museums Northern Ireland (NMNI); 56tr: Chitose Suzuki/AP Images; 56clt: Bedford Lemere & Co./National Maritime Museum, Greenwich, London/Royal Museums Greenwich; 56clb: White Star Photo Library; 56cr: RMS *Titanic*, Inc./AP Images; 56 (person icons): Leremy/Shutterstock; 56br: stocksnapper/iStockphoto; 56–57 (background): White Star Photo Library; 56–57 (Goodwin family): Wikipedia; 58cl: Eric Risberg/AP Images; 58bl: from Titanic*: Triumph and Tragedy*, 3rd edition, by John P. Eaton and Charles A. Haas; 58–59: Tim Loughhead/Precision Illustration; 59tr: Bain News Service/Flickr Commons Project 2011/Library of Congress; 59br: Harland & Wolff, Ulster Folk & Transport Museum/National Museums Northern Ireland (NMNI); 60l, 60cr: Science Source; 60br: White Star Photo Library; 61tl: Tom Gannam/AP Images; 61tcl: Wulfruna/iStockphoto; 61tcr: White Star Line/Wikipedia; 61tr: Father Browne/UIG/Science and Society Picture Library; 61b: Interfoto/Mary Evans Picture Library; 62ct: JordiRamisa/iStockphoto; 62cm: Jesus Cervantes/Shutterstock; 62cb: YinYang/iStockphoto; 62bc: Victor de Schwanberg/Science Source; 62br: White Star Photo Library; 62–63 (main image): Father Browne/Universal Images Group/Getty Images; 63bl: RM Auctions; 63bc: FourOaks/iStockphoto; 63br: dja65/iStockphoto; 64 (women icons): 4x6/iStockphoto; 64 (men icons): Leremy/Shutterstock; 64bc: F. M. Browne/Bettmann/Corbis Images; 64tr: Popperfoto/Getty Images; 64crt: White Star Photo Library; 64crb: Harland & Wolff, Ulster Folk & Transport Museum/National Museums Northern Ireland (NMNI); 64br: White Star Photo Library; 65 (bugle): Batman2000/iStockphoto; 65 (oysters): iStockphoto/Thinkstock; 65 (plates icon): studiocasper/iStockphoto; 65 (champagne icon): rzymu/iStockphoto; 65 (cup): RMS *Titanic*, Inc./AP Images; 65 (sports icons): DusanVulic/iStockphoto; 65 (piano icon): kathykonkle/iStockphoto; 65 (quoits): edhor/iStockphoto; 65 (books): Leadinglights/iStockphoto; 65 (accordion): Stockbyte/Thinkstock; 65 (lightbulb icon, family icons): bubaone/iStockphoto; 66–67: Father Browne/Universal Images Group/Getty Images; 68 (globes): SoleilC/Shutterstock; 68 (*Titanic* silhouette): Tim Loughhead/Precision Illustration; 68 (map): Nicemonkey/Shutterstock; 68bl, 68bc: Swansea Museum; 68br: George & Judy Manna/Science Source; 69tl: Hulton Archive/Stringer/Getty Images; 69 (binoculars): Bebeto Matthews/AP Images; 69bl: Steve Percival/Science Source; 69br: Alastair Grant/AP Images; ;70tl: Father Frank Browne/Wikipedia; 70tc: Ed Young/Science Source; 70tr: Harland & Wolff, Ulster Folk & Transport Museum/National Museums Northern Ireland (NMNI); 70bl: Hulton-Deutsch Collection/Corbis Images; 70–71 (*Titanic* silhouettes): Tim Loughhead/Precision Illustration; 71tc: Bebeto Matthews/AP Images; 71tr: farbenrausch/iStockphoto; 71 (sextant): Steve Percival/Science Source; 71 (iceberg cr): Logray-2008/iStockphoto; 71 (background ice): yienkeat/Shutterstock; 71 (Smith): White Star Photo Library; 71 (Ismay): Universal Images Group/Getty Images; 72l: Norman Gryspeerdt/ITV Global/The Picture Desk; 72c: Tim Loughhead/Precision Illustration; 72r: National Archives and Records Administration; 74–75: Bettmann/Corbis Images; 76–77 (*Titanic* silhouettes): Tim Loughhead/Precision Illustration; 76cm: DanielBendjy/iStockphoto; 76cr: W. Merie Wallace/20th Century Fox/Paramount/The Picture Desk; 77 (rocket explosion): Pilarts/Dreamstime; 77cm: Norman Gryspeerdt/ITV Global/The Picture Desk; 77cr: Father Browne/Universal Images Group/Getty Images; 78–79 (*Titanic* silhouettes): Tim Loughhead/Precision Illustration; 78cl: National Maritime Museum Picture Library/Royal Museums Greenwich; 78cm: Laures/iStockphoto; 79cl: Rama/Wikipedia; 80–81: National Archives and Records Administration; 82br: Wikipedia; 83tc: Photodisc/Thinkstock; 83tr: from *The Wireless Man* by Francis A. Collins, Grosset & Dunlap, New York, copyright 1912 by the Century Company/Wikipedia; 83bc, 83br: Father Browne/UIG/Science and Society Picture Library; 84–85 (all): Tim Loughhead/Precision Illustration; 86–87: Norman Gryspeerdt/ITV Global/The Picture Desk; 88l: Library of Congress; 88c: Stock Montage/Getty Images; 88r: Bain News Service/Flickr Commons Project 2012 and San Francisco Call, June 2, 1912/Library of Congress; 90–91 (main image): akg-images; 90tr, 91tl: Bettmann/Corbis Images; 91tc: English School/The Bridgeman Art Library/Getty Images; 91tr: George Grantham Bain Collection/Library of Congress; 91cr: Bain News Service/Flickr Commons Project 2012 and San Francisco Call, June 2, 1912/Library of Congress; 91br: Library of Congress; 92–93: Southampton City Council Arts & Heritage; 94 (Brown): George Grantham Bain Collection/Library of Congress; 94 (Lowe): Science Source; 94 (Collett): George Grantham Bain Collection/Library of Congress; 94bl: Topical Press Agency/Stringer/Getty Images; 94 (Collyers): Bain News Service/Flickr Commons Project 2012 and San Francisco Call, June 2, 1912/Library of Congress; 94 (Spedden): Father Browne/Universal Images Group/Getty Images; 94 (Gracie): Wikipedia; 94 (Harts): Eva Hart/AP Images; 94 (Fleet): Harris & Ewing Collection/Library of Congress; 94 (Boxhall): Wikipedia; 95 (man, woman, child icons): bubaone/iStockphoto; 95 (crew icon): Leremy/Shutterstock; 95 (Phillips): Father Browne/UIG/Science and Society Picture Library; 95 (Guggenheim): Wikipedia; 95 (Andrews): Harland & Wolff, Ulster Folk & Transport Museum/National Museums Northern Ireland (NMNI); 95 (Strauses): Wikipedia; 95 (musicians): Universal Images Group/Getty Images; 95 (Goodwins): Wikipedia; 95 (shoes): Wang Lei/Xinhua/Photoshot/Newscom; 95 (Sidney Goodwin): Wikipedia; 95 (March): from Titanic*: Triumph and Tragedy*, 3rd edition, by John P. Eaton and Charles A. Haas; 95 (Murdoch): Science Source; 95 (McElroy): White Star Photo Library; 96tr: The Graphic/Wikipedia; 96cl: Bain Collection/Library of Congress/Wikipedia; 96cm: Bassano & Vandyk Studios/National Portrait Gallery, London; 96cr: Wikipedia; 96–97b: Stock Montage/Getty Images; 97 (Ismay): Universal Images Group/Getty Images; 97 (Sir Duff Gordon): Topical Press Agency/Stringer/Getty Images; 97 (Lady Duff Gordon): George Grantham Bain Collection/Library of Congress; 97br: Bs0u10e01/Wikipedia; 98 (ice): Hulton Archive/Stringer/Getty Images; 98 (stamp): TonyBaggett/iStockphoto; 98 (*Titanic* silhouette): Tim Loughhead/Precision Illustration; 99tl: US Navy; 99tr: Wikipedia; 99br: Wikipedia; 100t: NOAA/Wikipedia; 100c: NOAA; 100bc: Bebeto Matthews/AP Images; 100br: RMS *Titanic*, Inc./AP Images; 100–101 (main image): NOAA; 101 (glasses): Bebeto Matthews/AP Images; 101 (gloves): Mary Altaffer/AP Images; 101bc: Bebeto Matthews/AP Images; 101br: NOAA; 102–103: NOAA/Institute for Exploration/University of Rhode Island (NOAA/IFE/URI)/Wikipedia; 104 (main image): Bain News Service/Flickr Commons Project 2008/Library of Congress; 104tr: Library of Congress; 105tl: Randy Bryan Bigham Collection/Wikipedia; 105tcl: Bain News Service/Flickr Commons Project 2011/Library of Congress; 105tcr: from *Methods and Players of Modern Lawn Tennis*, 1915, page 200/J. Parmley Paret/Wikipedia; 105tr: Stephen Daniels/Wikipedia; 105cm: from *The Day Book*, Chicago, April 19, 1912, page 23/Wikipedia; 105bl: Bain News Service/Library of Congress/Wikipedia; 105br: Father Browne/Universal Images Group/Getty Images; 106: White Star Photo Library; 107: Bebeto Matthews/AP Images; 108: Sang Tan/AP Images; all others: Scholastic Inc.

COVER

Front cover: Popperfoto/Getty Images. Back cover: (tr) Sang Tan/AP Images; (computer monitor) Manaemedia/Dreamstime.

Key to symbols in **More here** columns

Keywords for web searches · *Suggested reading* · *Movies and programmes to watch* · *Songs and recordings to listen to* · *Exciting places to visit* · *Great things to do* · *Mini-glossary*

Credits and acknowledgments